Latin American Literature
in English Translation

The Center for Inter-American Relations is a non-profit, membership organization conducting educational programs intended to provide U.S. citizens with greater understanding and awareness of the other nations in the Western Hemisphere. The Center's literature program has sponsored the translation of more than forty-five books, including works by such writers as Jorge Luis Borges, Gabriel García Márquez, Pablo Neruda, Julio Cortázar, José Donoso, Mario Vargas Llosa, Octavio Paz, Severo Sarduy, Manuel Puig, José Emilio Pacheco and Isabel Fraire.

Latin American Literature in English Translation

An Annotated Bibliography

Bradley A. Shaw

A Center for Inter-American Relations Book
Published by
New York University Press • New York • 1976

LIBRARY
University of Texas
At San Antonio

Library of Congress Cataloging in Publication Data

Shaw, Bradley A   1945-
    Latin American literature in English translation.

    Includes indexes.
    1. Latin American literature—Translations into English—Bibliography.
2. English literature—Translations from Spanish—Bibliography.   3. English
literature—Translations from Portuguese—Bibliography.   4. English
literature—Translations from French—Bibliography.   I. Title.
Z1609.T7S47   [PQ7087.E5]   016.86'008   75-7522
ISBN 0-8147-7762-7

Manufactured in the United States of America

Preface

It is hoped that this volume will be of assistance to students, teachers and scholars of Latin American literature, and to others whose profession or interest may lead them to seek information about the growing number of literary works from Latin America in English translation. In recent years that list has expanded greatly as contemporary Latin American writers receive more international attention and recognition. Of course there is much yet to be done, but there are encouraging signs that in the future the English-speaking world will have access to more and more competent translations of outstanding works.

To provide a practical and yet comprehensive guide to the literature of Latin America, the scope of the bibliography is limited to published books which include fiction, poetry, drama, or the literary essay in English translation. Collections which contain, but do not emphasize works from Latin America (such as anthologies of world literature) are generally excluded, unless they are worthy of mention for a still significant number of works. Periodical literature and literary criticism are not included in this study, and it is hoped that in the near future updated bibliographies of both will be made available. It should be noted, however, that books which originally appeared as special issues of or supplements to periodicals (such as *TriQuarterly*) and were then published separately are included because of their importance. Books are arranged according to language and culture, with anthologies followed by individual works which are listed alphabetically by country. This is designed so that teachers may more easily locate and select works for courses of Latin American literature in English translation. Anthologies containing selections from more than one language are generally included in each of the major sections for the literatures involved. Each separate bibliography is therefore more complete in itself and more practical to use.

Fortunately, at this time there are several excellent anthologies as well as major works of fiction and poetry (and recent collections of plays) which may be obtained in relatively inexpensive paperback editions. Included among the works of fiction, poetry and drama are selected essays, chosen because they are either of considerable literary merit or because they are written by leading figures in another genre. The number of essays is limited in the interest of maintaining the literary emphasis of the study, and avoiding an unwanted excursion into the realm of sociology, history, political science, philosophy, criticism, or other related areas of interest common to the essay.

Entries are annotated descriptively, that is, certain information is given about the contents or nature of the works that may be of help in developing a personal reading list for the student and general reader. Of scholarly interest are references to any significant textual changes (by the author or translator) in the original works or their translations. Also indicated are other important features of each book, such as glossaries, appendixes, and introductions. To evaluate every item critically is a task which would make a literary history of such an extensive list of books, although an attempt has been made to point out particularly significant works.

Entries are made for books published mainly in the United States and Great Britain before January 1, 1975. An asterisk following the item indicates that no American editions of the title are listed in *Books in Print* (1974). It should be noted that a few titles were unavailable for annotation, and that a few others may be omitted from the bibliography because of late announcements.

As one would expect, the Spanish American and Brazilian sections are most extensive. Not only are new titles added to the most recent bibliographical studies, but many corrections and additions are made to make this volume as accurate and complete as possible. Puerto Rican literature is also included here. The fact that Chicano literature, however, is not represented, does not mean that it is neither important nor extensive. It is felt, however, that only relatively few works meet the basic requirement for selection: that the work be a translation into English from another language. Many works, of course, combine both languages in a vital expression of personal and collective experiences and concerns. Bibliographical studies of journals including *El Grito* (Berkeley) and *Aztlán* (University of California at Los Angeles), and works such as Talbot and Cruz' *Chicano bibliography, 1960-1972* (Austin: Jenkins, 1973) should be consulted for references to Chicano literature.

A third section dealing with the literature in English translation from the Caribbean islands and the Guyanas is added to provide an even broader view of the literature of our hemisphere. This list relies heavily on Marjorie Engber's *Caribbean fiction and poetry* (New York: Center for Inter-American Relations, 1970), with additions and amendments by Elisha Trammell (Tram) Combs, Jr. and the compiler.

Two appendixes are also provided as guides for further reading in related fields. Both native American and Spanish colonial writings have been significant factors in molding the literature of Spanish America. The former is of considerable interest today considering the critical attention given to magical and mythical elements of writers such as Asturias, Carpentier, and others. Stress is given to works of literary interest, although a clear distinction between history and creative prose, or indigenous works of literary as opposed to anthropological or historical importance, is not easy to establish.

I wish to acknowledge the great debt owed to previous bibliographers whose studies have been indispensable in the compilation of this work. Several bibliographies by Willis Knapp Jones, a pioneer in the area of bibliographical research of Latin American literature and a noted translator and scholar, are invaluable. Of singular importance are his *Latin American Writers in English Translation* (Washington: Pan American Union, 1944; rpt. Detroit: Blaine Ethridge, 1972), *Latin America through drama in English* (Washington: Pan American Union, 1950), and "Spanish American Literature," in *The literatures of the world in English translation: A bibliography*, ed. George B. Parks and Ruth Z. Temple (New York: Ungar, 1970), III, pt. 1, pp. 329-453. The extensive work done by Professor Claude L. Hulet is the most complete of its kind. His *Latin American prose in English translation* (Washington: Pan American Union, 1964) and *Latin American poetry in English translation* (Washington: Pan American Union, 1965) are particularly significant for they include books and periodical literature. The most current bibliography of fiction and poetry is by noted translator Suzanne Jill Levine: *Latin America: Fiction and poetry in translation* (New York: Center for Inter-American Relations, 1970).

Brazilian works are included in the Jones, Hulet, and Levine bibliographies, although "Brazilian literature," comp. William Berrien, John M. Fein, and Benjamin M. Woodridge, Jr., rev. Benjamin M. Woodridge, Jr., in *The literatures of the world in English translation*, ed. Parks and Temple (New York: Ungar, 1970), III, pt. 1, pp. 193-212, *Brazil, Portugal, and other Portuguese-speaking lands; a list of books primarily in English*, comp. David T. Haberly and Francis M. Rogers (Cambridge: Harvard Univ. Pr., 1968), and compiler Georgette M. Dorn's *Latin America, Spain, and Portugal: An annotated bibliography of paperback books* (Washington: Library of Congress, 1971) are fairly recent works which provide further information.

Every effort has been made to verify the entries of these and other bibliographies, although at times this has not always been possible. Unfortunately certain publishing houses here and abroad fail to provide adequate bibliographical data about their books. Of course any errors and omissions in the bibliography are the sole responsibility of the compiler.

I wish to acknowledge my gratitude to Mr. Ronald Christ and Miss Rosario Santos of the Center for Inter-American Relations for their patience, encouragement, and support, and to Mrs. Eileen Hume, Mr. Joel Boone, Mr. Gilbert Shaw, and Mrs. Maria Smith for their helpful assistance. Among those whose interest and cooperation have been most appreciated are Mr. George C. Hart, Latin American bibliographer at the Ohio State University Library, Mr. Roberto Cabello-Argandoña, Director of the Chicano Research Library, University of California at Los Angeles, Dr. Mary Ellis Kabler, Chief of the Latin American, Portuguese, and Spanish Division, Library of Congress, the University Place Book Shop (New York City), and the staff of the reference and inter-library loan departments of Farrell Library, Kansas State University.

The assistance of Mr. Elisha Trammel (Tram) Combs, Jr. is most deeply appreciated and merits special recognition. The meticulous reading of the manuscript with many suggestions, corrections, and additions denote a high degree of professionalism and a profound interest and knowledge of the literature of all the languages of the region.

Most of all I wish to thank my wife Susan for her patience and many sacrifices throughout the duration of this rewarding, but often frustrating project.

Bradley A. Shaw

Kansas State University

Contents

I Spanish American Literature

A. Anthologies

1. Mixed Genre

1. Allen, John Houghton, comp. and tr. *A Latin-American miscellany.* Randado, Texas, 1943. 77 p.* Privately printed by the translator.

Appropriately called a "miscellany," for it includes selections from the colonial era, romanticism, modernism, and the postmodernist period.
Prose selections by: Rubén Darío (Nicaragua), José Eustasio Rivera (Colombia), Rufino Blanco Fombona (Venezuela), Ricardo Palma (Peru), José Enrique Rodó (Uruguay), Domingo Faustino Sarmiento (Argentina).
Poetry selections by: Fabio Fiallo (Dominican Republic), Sor Juana Inés de la Cruz (Mexico), Amado Nervo (Mexico), Enrique González Martínez (Mexico), Rubén Darío (Nicaragua), Aquileo J. Echeverría (Costa Rica), José Asunción Silva (Colombia), Emilio Gallegos del Campo (Ecuador), José Santos Chocano (Peru), Julio Herrera y Reissig (Uruguay), Enrique Banchs (Argentina), José Hernández (Argentina).
Also included are poems by

Gutierre de Cetina (Spain) and José-María de Hérédia (Cuba, from French), and an excerpt of a chronicle by Spanish conquistador Bernardino Vásquez de Tapia.

2. Babín, María Teresa and Stan Steiner, ed. *Borinquen; an anthology of Puerto Rican literature.* Tr. Barry Jay Luby. Intro. María Teresa Babín. New York: Knopf, 1974. 515 p. (rpt. New York: Vintage, 1974. paper)

An anthology of five centuries of Puerto Rican writing. Includes translations and selections from recent works written in English. Of interest is the section "Notes about contributors" (pp. 481-506).
Selections of prose fiction by: Ricardo E. Alegría, Cayetano Coll y Toste, Ramón Emetrio Betances, Manuel Zeno Gandía, Miguel Meléndez Muñoz, José Padín, César Andréu Iglesias, José I. de Diego Padró, Julio Marrero Nuñez, Enrique A. Laguerre, Antonio Oliver Frau, Wilfredo Braschi, Abelardo Díaz Alfaro, José Luis González, Luis Quero Chiesa, Jesús Colón, Piri Thomas, Víctor Hernández Cruz (prose poems).
Essays by: Eugenio María de Hostos, Nemesio R. Canales, Antonio S. Pedreira, María Teresa Babín, Concha Meléndez, Tomás

Blanco, Nilita Vientós Gastón, Luis Muñoz Rivera, Luis Muñoz Marín, José de Diego, Gilberto Concepción de Gracia, Pedro Albizu Campos, Samuel Betances.

Selections from plays by: Luis Lloréns Torres, Francisco Arriví, Manuel Méndez Ballester.

Poems by: Damián López de Haro, Juan Rodríguez Calderón, Santiago Vidarte, Luis Loréns Torres, Manuel A. Alonso, Lola Rodríguez de Tió, José Gautier Benítez, Francisco Alvarez Marrero, Pachín Marín, José Mercado, Luis Palés Matos, José A. Balseiro, José de Diego, Virgilio Dávila, José Antonio Dávila, Félix Franco Oppenheimer, Francisco Matos Paoli, Francisco Lluch Mora, Evaristo Ribera Chevremont, Julia de Burgos, Luis Hernández Aquino, Gustavo Agrait, Francisco Manrique Cabrera, Juan Avilés, Olga Ramírez de Arellano Nolla, José P. H. Hernández, Manuel Joglar Cacho, Juan Antonio Corretjer, Juan Martínez Capó, Jorge Luis Morales, Violeta López Suria, Diana Ramírez de Arellano, Clemente Soto Vélez, Andrés Castro Ríos, Roy Brown, Edwin Claudio, Jack Agüeros, Migdalia Rivera, Pedro Pietri, Father David García (with selections from a folk mass composed by the priest and his parishioners).

3. Brof, Janet and Hortense Carpentier, ed. and comp. *Doors and mirrors: Fiction and poetry from Spanish America, 1920-1970.* Intro. Angel Rama. Afterword Mario Vargas Llosa. New York: Grossman, 1972. xvi, 454 p. (rpt. New York: Viking Pr., 1973. 456 p. paper)

A very comprehensive and representative anthology of contemporary literature. Suitable for classroom use.

Includes short biographies of the writers and an index of translators.

Prose fiction selections by: Felisberto Hernández (Uruguay), Robert Arlt (Argentina), Miguel Angel Asturias (Guatemala), Jorge Luis Borges (Argentina) (2), Augusto Roa Bastos (Paraguay), Alejo Carpentier (Cuba), José María Arguedas (Peru), Juan Carlos Onetti (Uruguay), Juan Rulfo (Mexico), René Marqués (Puerto Rico), Gabriel García Márquez (Colombia), Adriano González León (Venezuela). Ricardo Ocampo (Bolivia), Daniel Moyano (Mexico), Enrique Lihn (Chile), José Lezama Lima (Cuba), Julio Cortázar (Argentina), Jaime Espinal (Colombia), Norberto Fuentes (Cuba), Antonio Skármeta (Chile).

Poetry selections (2 to 7) by: Vicente Huidobro (Chile), César Vallejo (Peru), Luis Palés Matos (Puerto Rico), Jorge Luis Borges (Argentina), Pablo Neruda (Chile), Nicolás Guillén (Cuba), José Coronel Urtecho (Nicaragua), Carlos Oquendo de Amat (Peru), Octavio Paz (Mexico), Cintio Vitier (Cuba), Nicanor Parra (Chile). Alvaro Mutis (Colombia), Ernesto Cardenal (Nicaragua), Sebastián Salazar Bondy (Peru), Roberto Juarroz (Argentina), Jaime Sabines (Mexico), Enrique Lihn (Chile), Roberto Fernández Retamar (Cuba), Ramón Palomares (Venezuela), Eduardo Escobar (Colombia), Juan Gelman (Argentina), Roque Dalton (El Salvador), Javier Heraud (Peru).

4. Cohen, J[ohn] M[ichael], ed. and intro. *Latin American writing today.* Harmondsworth & Baltimore: Penguin, 1967. 267 p. bibliog. paper (rpt. Gloucester, Mass.: Peter Smith, 1967. cloth)

Various translators, Bibliographical notes on the authors (pp. 261-267). Mostly new translations.

Well-chosen selections from the most outstanding writers of modern times.

Prose selections: Jorge Luis Borges (Argentina), Juan Carlos Onetti (Uruguay), Alejo Carpentier (Cuba), Julio Cortázar (Argentina), Carlos Fuentes (Mexico), Mario Benedetti (Uruguay), José Donoso (Chile), Juan Rulfo (Mexico), Gabriel García Márquez (Colombia), Guillermo Cabrera Infante (Cuba), Onelio Jorge Cardoso (Cuba).

Poems (no more than 4 by an individual) by: Gabriela Mistral (Chile), César Vallejo (Peru), Ricardo E. Molinari (Argentina), Pablo Neruda (Chile), Carlos Pellicer (Mexico), Octavio Paz (Mexico), Rosario Castellanos (Mexico), Alí Chumacero (Mexico), Nicanor Parra (Chile), Alberto Girri (Argentina), Jaime Sabines (Mexico), Pablo Armando Fernández (Cuba), Enrique Lihn (Chile), José Emilio Pacheco (Mexico), Marco Antonio Montes de Oca (Mexico).

This volume also includes works by Brazilians. See No. 415.

5. Cohen, J[ohn] M[ichael], ed. and intro. *Writers in the new Cuba; an anthology.* Harmondsworth & Baltimore: Penguin, 1967. 191 p. paper (rpt. Gloucester, Mass.: Peter Smith, 1967, cloth).

Nicely done. Works from the post-1959 era are chosen primarily for literary merit.

Includes poems by: Roberto Fernández Retamar, Heberto Padilla, Fayad Jamís, Pablo Armando Fernández, Luis Marré, José Alvarez Baragaño, Rolando Rigali, Domingo Alfonso.

Short stories by: Calvert Casey, Onelio Jorge Cardoso, Virgilio Piñera, Humberto Arenal, Ana María Simo (2), Rogelio Llopis, Guillermo Cabrera Infante, Jesús Díaz Rodríguez, Luis Agüero, Reynaldo González.

Contains a one-act play by Abelardo Estorino.

The volume is concluded with excerpts from a speech by Fidel Castro: "Words to the intellectuals" (June, 1961).

6. Coulthard, G.R., ed., tr. and intro. *Caribbean literature; an anthology.* London: Univ. of London Pr., 1966. 128 p.

Most of the selections are from English-speaking writers.

Includes poems by Nicolás Guillén (Cuba) and Luis Palés Matos (Puerto Rico); short stories by René Marqués (Puerto Rico) and Enrique Serpa (Cuba).

Also includes selections translated from French. See No. 525.

7. Cranfill, Thomas Mabry and George D. Schade, ed. *The muse in Mexico; a mid-century miscellany.* Austin: Univ. of Texas Pr., 1959. x, 117 p. [63] p. photographs, illus.

Issued as a supplement to *Texas Quarterly,* II, No. 1, but a book in itself. Various translators. Translations edited by George D. Schade. Includes photographs of 16 creative artists of Mexico, by Hans Beachan.

A nice introduction to Mexican art and letters of the period.

Prose fiction selections by: Juan de la Cabada, Juan José Arreola (2), Juan Rulfo (2), Guadalupe Amor, José Vasconcelos, Emilio Carballido, Guadalupe Dueñas, Julio Torri.

Poetry selections include 3 Aztec poems, 3 Nahuatl poems. Poets represented: Rosario Castellanos, Juan José Tablada, Enrique Rivas, Francisco González Guerrero, Alí Chumacero, Manuel Durán, Neftalí Beltrán, Rubén Bonifaz Nuño, Jaime Sabines, Tomás Segovia, Carlos Pellicer, Octavio Paz.

Unpaged section includes 61 drawings by Siqueiros, Orozco, Tamayo, Rivera, Castro Pacheco, Dr. Atl.

8. Flakoll, Darwin J. and Claribel Alegría, ed., tr., and intro. *New voices of Hispanic America; an anthology.* Boston: Beacon Pr., 1962. 226 p.*

Includes a variety of selections from widely recognized and lesser-known writers. Uneven in quality of works, but a particularly important contribution at the time of publication.

The original text of the poems is included with the translations.

Short stories by: José Donoso (Chile), Augusto Monterroso (Guatemala), Juan Rulfo (Mexico), Augusto Roa Bastos (Paraguay), Porfirio Meneses (Peru), Sebastián Salazar Bondy (Peru), René Marqués (Puerto Rico), Mario Benedetti (Uruguay), Antonio Márquez Salas (Venezuela), Julio Cortázar (Argentina), Juan José Arreola (Mexico).

Poems by: Eduardo Anguita (Chile), Rubén Bonifaz Nuño (Mexico), Ernesto Cardenal (Nicaragua), Alfredo Cardona Peña (Costa Rica), Rosario Castellanos (Mexico), Carlos Castro Saavedra (Colombia), Elba Fábregas (Argentina), Otto Raúl González (Guatemala), Ida Gramcko (Venezuela), Dora Guerra (El Salvador), Fayad Jamís (Cuba),

Enrique Lihn (Chile), Hugo Lindo (El Salvador), Ernesto Mejía Sánchez (Nicaragua), H. A. Murena (Argentina), Alberto Ordóñez Argüello (Nicaragua), Adalberto Ortiz (Ecuador), Nicanor Parra (Chile), Joaquín Pasos (Nicaragua), Octavio Paz (Mexico), Gonzalo Rojas (Chile), José Guillermo Ross Zanet (Panama), Alberto Rubio (Chile), Hugo Salazar Tamariz (Ecuador), Nivaria Tejera (Cuba), Blanca Varela (Peru), Idea Vilariño (Uruguay), Ida Vitale (Uruguay), Cintio Vitier (Cuba), María Elena Walsh (Argentina).

This anthology also includes works by other poets.

9. Howes, Barbara, ed. *From the green Antilles.* New York: Macmillan, 1966. 368 p. *

Includes selections of prose and poetry from the English-speaking West Indies and translations from Spanish, French, Dutch. Spanish Americans included are: Emilio S. Belaval (Puerto Rico), Tomás Blanco (Puerto Rico), Juan Bosch (Dominican Republic), Lydia Cabrera (Cuba), Alejo Carpentier (Cuba), Abelardo Díaz Alfaro (Puerto Rico), Eliseo Diego (Cuba), Nicolás Guillén (Cuba), Carlos Montenegro (Cuba), Lino Novás Calvo (Cuba), Pedro Juan Soto (Puerto Rico).

Many translators.

10. Jones, Willis Knapp, ed. and intro. *Spanish American literature in translation: A selection of prose, poetry, and drama before 1888.* Vol. I. New York: Frederick Ungar, 1966. xv, 356 p. bibliog.

The second of a two volume anthology of selected writings. The volume of modern literature was published first. See No. 11. Many translators.

Provides a broad overview of the literature, with introductory material and notes.

Selections include fragments from the Maya-Quiché *Popol Vuh*, Inca and Nahuatl poems, and selections from the writings of Cristóbal Colón, Hernando Cortés, and Bartolomé de Las Casas of Spain. Other Spanish writers who wrote and lived in America are listed according to the country described in their works.

Prose selections are by: José de Acosta (Peru), Ignacio Manuel Altamirano (Mexico), Fray Bernardino de Sahagún (Mexico), Alberto Blest Gana (Chile), Simón Bolívar (Venezuela), Pedro Cieza de León (Peru), Concolorcorvo [Alonso Carrió de la Vandera], Bernal Díaz del Castillo (Mexico), Ruiz Díaz de Guzmán (Paraguay), Esteban Echeverría (Argentina), José Joaquín Fernández de Lizardi (Mexico), Manuel de Jesús Galván (Dominican Republic), Inca Garcilaso de la Vega (Peru), Jorge Isaacs (Colombia), Diego de Landa (Mexico), José Mármol (Argentina), Clorinda Matto de Turner (Peru), Juan León Mera (Ecuador), Bartolomé Mitre (Argentina), Juan Montalvo (Ecuador), Motolinía [Fray Toribio de Benavente] (Mexico), Francisco Morazán (Honduras), Alvar Núñez Cabeza de Vaca (Mexico), Francisco Núñez de Pineda y Bascuñán (Chile), Alonso de Ovalle (Chile), Ricardo Palma (Peru), Manuel Payno (Mexico), Vicente Pérez Rosales (Chile), Domingo Faustino Sarmiento (Argentina), Carlos de Sigüenza y Góngora (Mexico), Cirilo Villaverde (Cuba).

Selections of poetry by: Manuel Acuña (Mexico), "Amarilis" (Peru), Olegario Víctor Andrade (Argentina), Bernardo de Balbuena (Mexico), Andrés Bello (Venezuela), Estanislao del Campo (Argentina), José Eusebio Caro (Colombia), Juan Cruz Varela (Argentina), Esteban Echeverría (Argentina), Alonso de Ercilla y Zúñiga (Chile), José Gautier Benítez (Puerto - Rico), Gertrudis Gómez de Avellaneda (Cuba), José María Heredia (Cuba), Sor Juana Inés de la Cruz (Mexico), Joaquín Lorenzo Luaces (Cuba), José Jacinto Milanés y Fuentes (Cuba), Rafael Obligado (Argentina), José Joaquín de Olmedo (Ecuador), Pedro de Oña (Chile), Juan Gualberto Padilla (Puerto Rico), "Plácido" (Cuba), Rafael Pombo (Colombia), Mariano Ramallo (Bolivia), Salvador Sanfuentes (Chile), Francisco de Terrazas (Mexico), Juan Zorrilla de San Martín (Uruguay).

Selections of drama by: Carlos Bello (Chile), Gertrudis Gómez de Avellaneda (Cuba), Sor Juana Inés de la Cruz (Mexico), Camilo Henríquez (Chile), Jerónimo de Monforte y Vera (Peru), José Peón y Contreras (Mexico), Ramón Vial y Ureta (Chile). In addition, fragments from 3 Indian dramas from Peru, Mexico, and Guatemala, and one anonymous play (Argentina) are included.

The volume is completed by a bibliography of works in English translation (pp. 345-351) and an index.

11. Jones, Willis Knapp, ed. and intro. *Spanish American literature in translation: A selection of prose, poetry, and drama since 1888*. Vol. II. New York: Frederick Ungar, 1963. xxi, 469 p. bibliog.

Various translators. The volume includes a bibliography ("A reading list'') and an index.

A comprehensive selection up to but not including the "new" generation of writers. Stresses the modernist and post-modernist periods.

Prose selections by: Eduardo Acevedo Díaz (Uruguay), Demetrio Aguilera Malta (Ecuador), Ciro Alegría (Peru), Rafael Arévalo Martínez (Guatemala), Alcides Arguedas (Bolivia), Mariano Azuela (Mexico), Eduardo Barrios (Chile), Rufino Blanco Fombona (Venezuela), Alberto Blest Gana (Chile), Jorge Luis Borges (Argentina), Marta Brunet (Chile), José Antonio Campos (Ecuador), Rómulo Gallegos (Venezuela), Ricardo Güiraldes (Argentina), Martín Luis Guzmán (Mexico), Jorge Icaza (Ecuador), Enrique Larreta (Argentina), Carmen Lyra (Costa Rica), Gregorio López y Fuentes (Mexico), Eduardo Mallea (Argentina), Rafael Maluenda Labarca (Chile), Enrique Méndez Calzada (Argentina), Amado Nervo (Mexico), Angel Pino (Chile), Pedro Prado (Chile), Horacio Quiroga (Uruguay), José Eustasio Rivera (Colombia), José Enrique Rodó (Uruguay), Froylán Turcios (Honduras), César Uribe Piedrahita (Colombia), Hugo Wast (Argentina).

Selections of poetry by: Lino Argüello (Nicaragua), Santiago Argüello Barreto (Nicaragua), Enrique Banchs (Argentina), Jorge Luis Borges (Argentina), Herib Campos Cervera (Paraguay), Jorge Carrera Andrade (Ecuador), Julián del Casal (Cuba), José Santos Chocano (Peru), Stella Corvalán (Chile), Rubén Darío (Nicaragua), Salvador Díaz Mirón (Mexico), Jorge Escobar Uribe (Argentina), Jacinto Fombona Pachano (Venezuela), Eloy Fariña Núñez (Paraguay), Fabio

Fiallo (Dominican Republic), Gastón Figueira (Uruguay), Enrique González Martínez (Mexico), Manuel González Prada (Peru), Alejandro Guanes (Paraguay), Nicolás Guillén (Cuba), Manuel Gutiérrez Nájera (Mexico), Juan Guzmán Cruchaga (Chile), Enrique Hernández Miyares (Cuba), Julio Herrera y Reissig (Uruguay), Vicente Huidobro (Chile), Juana de Ibarbourou (Uruguay), Ricardo Jaimes Freyre (Bolivia), Claudia Lars (El Salvador), Luis Lloréns Torres (Puerto Rico), Luis Carlos López (Colombia), Ramón López Velarde (Mexico), Leopoldo Lugones (Argentina), José Martí (Cuba), Gabriela Mistral (Chile), Guillermo Molinas Rolón (Paraguay), Pablo Neruda (Chile), Amado Nervo (Mexico), Juan E. O'Leary (Paraguay), Miguel Angel Osorio (Colombia), Luis Palés Matos (Puerto Rico), Octavio Paz (Mexico), Regino Pedroso (Cuba), Josefina Pla (Paraguay), Alfonso Reyes (Mexico), Augusto Roa Bastos (Paraguay), Elvio Romero (Paraguay), Cesáreo Rosa-Nieves (Puerto Rico), José Asunción Silva (Colombia), Medaro Angel Silva (Ecuador), Alfonsina Storni (Argentina), César Tiempo (Argentina), Jaime Torres Bodet (Mexico), Froylán Turcios (Honduras), Guillermo Valencia (Colombia), César Vallejo (Peru), Julio Vicuña Cifuentes (Chile).

Drama selections by: Antonio Acevedo Hernández (Chile), Isidora Aguirre (Chile), Carlos S. Damel (Argentina), Camilo Darthés (Argentina), Samuel Eichelbaum (Argentina), José Joaquín Gamboa (Mexico), Eduardo Gutiérrez (Argentina), René Marqués (Puerto Rico), Armando Moock (Chile), Francisco Navarro (Mexico), Pedro E. Pico (Argentina), José J. Podestá (Argentina), José Antonio Ramos (Cuba), José María Rivarola Matto (Paraguay), Florencio Sánchez (Uruguay), Rodolfo Usigli (Mexico).

12. Kaiden, Nina E., Pedro Juan Soto and Andrew Vladimer, ed. *Puerto Rico: La nueva vida. The new life.* New York: Renaissance Editions, 1966. 1 vol. unpaged [94 p.] plates.

Brief selections of contemporary prose, poetry and art. Various translators. Bilingual text in parallel format. Plates of contemporary paintings (33) are included throughout the text.

Prose (including fragments) by: Emilio S. Belaval, Salvador M. de Jesús, José Luis González, Ramón Julia Marín, Edwin Figueroa, Luis Hernández Aquino, Juan Antonio Corretjer, María Teresa Babín, René Marqués, Emilio Díaz Valcárcel, Margot Arce de Vásquez, Tomás Blanco, Pedro Juan Soto.

Poems by: Clara Lair, Hugo Margenat, Carmen Alicia Cadilla, José P. H. Hernández, Luis Lloréns Torres, Luis Palés Matos, Luis Muñoz Rivera, José de Jesús Esteves, Tomás Blanco, Guillermo Atiles García, Carmen Puigdollers, José de Diego, Julia de Burgos.

13. *Literature in Latin America.* Washington, D.C.: Pan American Union, 1950. 112p.*

Brief selections of twentieth-century writers. The essays deal primarily with aspects of Latin American culture.

Selections of prose fiction by: Juan Pablo Echaque (Argentina), Manuel González Zeledón (Costa Rica), Virgilio Díaz Ordóñez (Dominican Republic), Gregorio López y Fuentes (Mexico), Ricardo Palma (Peru), Julián Padrón (Venezuela).

Poetry selections by: Leopoldo Lugones (Argentina), Gabriela Mistral (Chile), Rafael Pombo (Colombia), José Asunción Silva (Colombia), Guillermo Valencia (Colombia), Enrique González Martínez (Mexico), Amado Nervo (Mexico), Justo Sierra (Mexico), Rubén Darío (Nicaragua), José Santos Chocano (Peru), Gastón Figueira (Uruguay), Julio Herrera y Reissig (Uruguay), Juana de Ibarbourou (Uruguay), Andrés Bello (Venezuela).

Essays by: Germán Arciniegas (Colombia), Antonio Gómez Restrepo (Colombia), José Gabriel Navarro (Ecuador), Rubén Darío (Nicaragua), Ricardo Joaquín Alfaro (Peru), Jorge Basadre (Peru), Héctor David Castro (El Salvador), Gabriela Mistral (Chile), Carlos Acuña (Bolivia), F. Castillo Nájera (Mexico), Luisa Luisi (Uruguay).

14. *The literature of Latin America.* Washington, D.C.: Pan American Union, 1942. iii, 64 p. *

Mostly reprints from the *Bulletin* of the Pan American Union. Various translators.

Short selections from mostly romantic and modernist writers. Not particularly representative of their best production.

Prose selections (fiction, descriptive prose, essays) by: José S. Alvarez (Argentina), Leopoldo Lugones (Argentina), Gabriel René-Moreno (Bolivia), Gabriela Mistral (Chile), Daniel Samper Ortega (Colombia), Manuel González Zeledón (Costa Rica), José Martí (Cuba), Pedro Henríquez Ureña (Dominican Republic), Juan Montalvo (Ecuador), Arturo Ambrogi (El Salvador), José Rodríguez Cerna (Guatemala), Marco Aurelio Soto (Honduras), Genaro Estrada (Mexico), Rubén Darío (Nicaragua), Ricardo J. Alfaro (Panama), Pablo Alborno (Paraguay), José Gálvez (Peru), Ricardo Palma (Peru), Juan Zorrilla de San Martín (Uruguay), Teresa de la Parra (Venezuela).

Poems by: Leopoldo Lugones (Argentina), José Asunción Silva (Colombia), Gabriela Mistral (Chile), Guillermo Valencia (Colombia), Amado Nervo (Mexico), Alfredo Gómez Jaime (Colombia), Luis G. Urbina (Mexico), Ricardo Palma (Peru), Osvaldo Bazil (Dominican Republic), Rufino Blanco Fombona (Venezuela), José María Heredia (Cuba), Enrique González Martínez (Mexico), José Santos Chocano (Peru), Rubén Darío (Nicaragua), Antonio Nicolás Blanco (Puerto Rico), Juana de Ibarbourou (Uruguay), Rafael Pombo (Colombia), Juan Zorrilla de San Martín (Uruguay), Sor Juana Inés de la Cruz (Mexico).

Also includes three Brazilian selections. See No. 416.

15. Miller, James E., Jr., Robert O'Neal and Helen M. McDonnell, ed. *From Spain and the Americas; literature in translation.* Intro. Angel Flores. New York: Scott, Foresman, 1970. 420 p. *

The intro. (pp. 9-16) includes a reading list of works in English translation. Also included are biographical sketches of the authors (pp. 410-414) and indices of authors, titles, and translators. The text is designed for high school use, with discussion questions and ample notes. Book divided into Spanish and Spanish American sections.

Short stories by: Ciro Alegría (Peru), Armando Arriaza [pseud.

Hermes Nahuel] (Chile), Jorge Luis Borges (Argentina), Jesús del Corral (Colombia), Juan Carlos Dávalos (Argentina), Marco Denevi (Argentina), Carlos Fuentes (Mexico), Gabriel García Márquez (Colombia), Horacio Quiroga (Uruguay), Luis Tablanca [Enrique Pardo Farelo] (Colombia), José Vasconcelos (Mexico).

Poems (2 to 6) by: Jorge Carrera Andrade (Ecuador), Jorge Luis Borges (Argentina), Pablo Antonio Cuadra (Nicaragua), Gastón Figueira (Uruguay), Gabriela Mistral (Chile), Pablo Neruda (Chile) [with one essay], Alfonsina Storni (Argentina), "César Tiempo" [Israel Zeitlin] (Argentina), Fernán Silva Valdés (Uruguay), César Vallejo (Peru).

Includes short story by Brazilian José Bento Monteiro Lobato.

16. Onís, Harriet de, ed., tr., and foreword. *The golden land; an anthology of Latin American folklore in literature.* New York: Knopf, 1948. xviii, 395 p. (rpt. 1971)

Not really a study of folklore. Selections of intrinsic literary value are chosen for information they provide about the land and the people. Many informative notes and biographical sketches.

Prose selections by Garcilaso de la Vega, el Inca (Peru), Fernando de Alva Ixtlilxochitl (Mexico), Juan Rodríguez Freile (Colombia), Antonio de la Calancha (Peru), Luis Lasso de la Vega (Mexico), José de Oviedo y Baños (Venezuela), Bartolomé Martínez y Vela (Bolivia), Francisco Javier Clavijero (Mexico), Gertrudis Gómez de Avellaneda (Cuba), Domingo F. Sarmiento (Argentina), Ricardo Palma (Peru), Tomás Carrasquilla (Colombia),

Javier de Viana (Uruguay), Manuel Bernardez (Uruguay), Roberto J. Payró (Argentina), Ricardo Rojas (Argentina), Alberto Gerchunoff (Argentina), Ricardo Güiraldes (Argentina), Jorge Luis Borges (Argentina), Germán Arciniegas (Colombia), Alcides Arguedas (Bolivia), Enrique López Albújar (Peru), Ventura García Calderón (Peru), Ciro Alegría (Peru), Mariano Latorre (Chile), Rómulo Gallegos (Venezuela), Arturo Uslar Pietri (Venezuela), Mariano Picón-Salas (Venezuela). Juan Bosch (Dominican Republic), Carlos Samayoa Chinchilla (Guatemala), Salvador Salazar Arrué (El Salvador), Carmen Lyra (Costa Rica), Martín Luis Guzmán (Mexico), Alfonso Reyes (Mexico).

Poetry selections by Estanislao del Campo (Argentina) and José Hernández (Argentina)

Also included are six prose selections from Spanish chronicles of the conquest, fragments of the Maya-Quiché *Popol Vuh,* and examples of popular literature (the Mexican *corridos*).

For Brazilian writers see No. 425.

17. *(TriQuarterly). The 'Tri-Quarterly' anthology of contemporary Latin American literature.* Ed. José Donoso and William A. Henkin, with the staff of *TriQuarterly.* New York: E.P. Dutton, 1969. xi, 496 p. illus.

Appeared originally as an issue of *TriQuarterly* (1969), but published and distributed separately in book form. This is an outstanding collection of works by established and developing writers. A most valuable contribution to the body of Latin American works in English translation.

Contains critical essays by Octavio

Paz (Mexico) and Emir Rodríguez Monegal (Uruguay).

Poems by César Vallejo (Peru), Javier Heraud (Peru), Octavio Paz (Mexico), Carlos Germán Belli (Peru), Pablo Neruda (Chile), Enrique Lihn (Chile), Carlos Castro Saavedra (Colombia), Rafael Pineda (Venezuela), Enrique Molina (Argentina), Marco Antonio Montes de Oca (Mexico), José Emilio Pacheco (Mexico), Jorge Luis Borges (Argentina), Nicanor Parra (Chile).

Other poets included in article-length anthologies:

"An anthology of Cuban poetry" (ed. Margaret Randall), with poems by Eliseo Diego, José Lezama Lima, Roberto Fernández Retamar, Fayad Jamís, Heberto Padilla, Pablo Armando Fernández, Miguel Barnet;

"An anthology of Peruvian poetry" (ed. Maureen Ahern Maurer), with selections by Antonio Cisneros, Wáshington Delgado, Julio Ortega, César Calvo, Juan Gonzalo Rose;

"An anthology of Argentine poetry" (ed. Patrick Morgan), with poems by Horacio Salas, Carlos J. Moneta, Armando Tejada Gómez, Miguel Grinberg, Leopoldo Marechal, Máximo Simpson, Edgar Bayley, Juan Gelman, Miguel Angel Bustos;

"Nine Paraguayan poets" (ed. Rubén Bareiro Saguier), with works by Esteban Cabañas, Ramiro Domínguez, René Dávalos, José Luis Appleyard, Francisco Pérez Maricevich, Rubén Bareiro Saguier, José María Gómez Sanjurjo, Adolfo Ferreiro, Roque Vallejos;

"An anthology of Mexican poetry" (ed. Margaret Randall), with poems by Octavio Paz, Isabel Fraire, Joaquín Sánchez MacGregor, Homero Aridjis, Sergio Mondragón,

Juan Bañuelos;

"An anthology of Chilean poetry" (ed. Alfonso Calderón), with selections by Efraín Barquero, Alberto Rubio, Gonzalo Rojas, Gonzalo Millán, Oscar Hahn, Jorge Teillier, Miguel Arteche.

Prose selections by Ernesto Sábato (Argentina), Gustavo Sáinz (Venezuela), Mario Vargas Llosa (Peru), Juan José Arreola (Mexico), Gabriel García Márquez (Colombia), Jorge Luis Borges (Argentina), Basilia Papastamatíu (Argentina), José Donoso (Chile), Juan José Hernández (Argentina), Vicente Leñero (Mexico), Miguel Angel Asturias (Guatemala), Julio Cortázar (Argentina), Carlos Fuentes (Mexico), Carlos Martínez Moreno (Uruguay).

Brazilian prose fiction also included. See No. 417.

18. Williams, Miller, ed. and tr. *Chile; an anthology of new writing.* Kent, Ohio: Kent State Univ. Pr., 1968. 1 vol. unpaged. illus.

Well-chosen selections from the sixties.

Includes poems by: Miguel Arteche, Efraín Barquero, Rolando Cárdenas, Luisa Johnson, Enrique Lihn, Pablo Neruda, Alberto Rubio, Jorge Teillier, Armando Uribe Arce.

Short stories by Antonio Skármeta and Poli Délano; a play by Raúl Ruíz.

The translations of the poems face the original texts in Spanish.

2. Prose

19. Arciniegas, Germán, ed. *The green continent: A comprehensive view of Latin America by its leading writers.* Tr. Harriet de Onís *et al.* New York: Knopf, 1944, xiii, 533 p. (rpt. London: Editions Poetry, 1947. 483 p.)*

Includes a variety of selections from important novels, short stories, historical, and literary essays from the first half of the twentieth century.

Selections by: Ciro Alegría (Peru), Alcides Arguedas (Bolivia), Benjamín Carrión (Ecuador), Gregorio Castañeda Aragón (Colombia), Augusto Céspedes (Bolivia), Genaro Estrada (Mexico), Rómulo Gallegos (Venezuela), Martín Luis Guzmán (Mexico), Flavio Herrera (Guatemala), Mariano Latorre (Chile), Leopoldo Lugones (Argentina), Jorge Mañach (Cuba), Juan Meléndez (Peru), Jules Mancini (Colombia), Juan Marín (Chile), Gabriela Mistral (Chile), José Nucete Sardi (Venezuela), Victoria Ocampo (Argentina), Juan E. O'Leary (Paraguay), Raúl Porras Barrenechea (Peru), Alfonso Reyes (Mexico), Julio Rinaldini (Argentina), Ricardo Rojas (Argentina), José Enrique Rodó (Uruguay), José Eustasio Rivera (Colombia), Baldomero Sanín Cano (Colombia), Domingo Faustino Sarmiento (Argentina), Armando Solano (Colombia), José Vasconcelos (Mexico).

For Brazilian writers, see No. 418.

20. [Carranza, Sylvia] and [María Juana Cazabon], ed. *Cuban short stories,* 1959-1966. Havana: Book Institute, 1967. 229 p. glossary, illus.

Many stories from revolutionary Cuba. Stories chosen for literary merit and documentary nature. A must for students of contemporary Cuba.

Selections by: Félix Pita Rodríguez, Virgilio Piñera, Samuel Feijóo, Víctor Agostini, Onelio Jorge Cardoso, Raúl Aparicio, Oscar Hurtado, Dora Alonso, Humberto Arenal, José Lorenzo Fuentes, Jesús

Díaz Rodríguez, Angel Arango, Miguel Collazo, Ezequiel Vieta, Antón Arrufat, Raúl González de Cascorro, Luis Agüero, María Elena Llana, Rogelio Llopis, Evora Tamayo, Arnaldo Correa, Ana María Simo, Reinaldo González, David Camps.

21. Colford, William E., ed. and tr. *Classic tales from Spanish America.* Woodbury, N.Y.: Barron, 1962. 210 p. paper.

A representative selection of early and mid-twentieth century stories.

Includes short stories by: Manuel Rojas (Chile), Eduardo Barrios (Chile), Baldomero Lillo (Chile), Ricardo Jaimes Freyre (Bolivia), Ricardo Palma (Peru), Héctor Velarde (Peru), Leopoldo Lugones (Argentina), Alberto Gerchunoff (Argentina), Rubén Darío (Nicaragua), Gonzalo Mayas Garbayo (Colombia), Enrique Serpa (Cuba), Rafael Bernal (Mexico), Gregorio López y Fuentes (Mexico), Amado Nervo (Mexico), Cayetano Coll y Toste (Puerto Rico), Abelardo Díaz Alfaro (Puerto Rico), Horacio Quiroga (Uruguay), Javier de Viana (Uruguay), Arturo Uslar Pietri (Venezuela).

22. Flores, Angel and Dudley Poore, ed. *Fiesta in November; stories from Latin America.* Intro. Katherine Anne Porter. Boston: Houghton Mifflin, 1942. 608 p.*

A fine collection of novels and short stories by Spanish American and Brazilian writers. Various translators.

An important contribution to the bibliography of works in translation at the time of publication. Uneven quality of selections, however.

For Brazilian entires, see No. 419.
Novels:
Aguilera Malta, Demetrio (Ecuador). *Don Goyo.* Frag. tr. Enid Eder Parkins. (*Don Goyo,* 1933)
Barrios, Eduardo (Chile). *Brother Ass.* Tr. R. Selden Rose and Francisco Aguilera. (see No. 102)
Mallea, Eduardo (Argentina). *Fiesta in November.* Tr. Alis de Sola. (*Fiesta en noviembre,* 1938)
Romero, José Rubén (Mexico). *The futile life of Pito Pérez.* Tr. Joan Coyne. See No. 188.
Short stories by: José Diez-Canseco (Peru), Luis Tablanca (Colombia), Guillermo Meneses (Venezuela), Héctor I. Eandi (Argentina), Horacio Quiroga (Uruguay), Rogelio Sinán (Panama), Juan Carlos Dávalos (Argentina), Arturo Uslar Pietri (Venezuela), Abraham Valdelomar (Peru), Adolfo Costa du Rels (Bolovia), Salvador Reyes (Chile), Rafael Maluenda Labarca (Chile), Armando Arriaza (Chile).

23. Flores, Angel, ed. and intro. *Great Spanish short stories.* New York: Dell, 1962. 304 p. paper.

The early twentieth-century selections from Latin America are overshadowed by the wider range of Spanish peninsular stories.

Includes works by Gregorio López y Fuentes (Mexico), Ricardo Palma (Peru), and Hernando Téllez (Colombia), with selections by Spanish authors.

24. Franco, Jean, ed. and intro. *Short stories in Spanish. Cuentos hispánicos.* Harmondsworth & Baltimore: Penguin, 1966. 204 p. paper

A noteworthy collection of outstanding stories by leading contemporary authors.

Bilingual edition, parallel texts. Of interest are the "Biographical notes on authors," pp. 191-195, and "Notes on Spanish texts," pp. 197-204. Various translators.

Of eight writers, only one is Spanish (Camilo José Cela).

Spanish American authors are: Mario Benedetti (Uruguay), Jorge Luis Borges (Argentina), Gabriel García Márquez (Colombia), Carlos Martínez Moreno (Uruguay), Juan Carlos Onetti (Uruguay), Juan Rulfo (Mexico), and H. A. Murena (Argentina).

25. Frank, Waldo, ed. *Tales from the Argentine.* Tr. Anita Brenner. New York: Farrar and Rinehart, 1930. xvi, 268p. (rpt. Freeport, N.Y.: Books for Libraries Pr., 1970)

Works from the nineteenth and early twentieth centuries.

Stories by Domingo Faustino Sarmiento, Lucio Vicente López, Roberto J. Payró, Leopoldo Lugones, Ricardo Güiraldes, and Horacio Quiroga (Uruguay).

26. Howes, Barbara, ed. *The eye of the heart; short stories from Latin America.* Indianapolis & New York: Bobbs-Merrill, 1973. xiv, 415 p. (rpt. New York: Avon, 1974.)

Stories of Spanish American and Brazilian authors. Selections are arranged chronologically, from 1882 to recent times. Of use are the "Notes on the contributors," pp. 403-412, and "Notes on the translators," pp. 413-415. An excellent edition, well suited for a college text. Good translations by various translators.

Spanish American writers represen-

ted are: Rubén Darío (Nicaragua), Leopoldo Lugones (Argentina), Horacio Quiroga (Uruguay), Rómulo Gallegos (Venezuela), Ricardo Güiraldes (Argentina), Gabriela Mistral (Chile), Alfonso Reyes (Mexico), César Vallejo (Peru), Jorge Luis Borges (Argentina), Miguel Angel Asturias (Guatemala), Roberto Arlt (Argentina), Alejo Carpentier (Cuba), Pablo Neruda (Chile) (recollections), Lino Novás-Calvo, (Cuba), Arturo Uslar Pietri (Venezuela), Juan Carlos Onetti (Uruguay), Juan Bosch (Dominican Republic), María Luisa Bombal (Chile), José María Arguedas (Peru), Julio Cortázar (Argentina), Octavio Paz (Mexico), Adolfo Bioy Casares (Argentina), Augusto Roa Bastos (Paraguay), Juan Rulfo (Mexico), Armonía Somers (Uruguay), Juan José Arreola (Mexico), Eliseo Diego (Cuba), Abelardo Díaz Alfaro (Puerto Rico), Humberto Costantini (Argentina), José Donoso (Chile), Gabriel García Márquez (Colombia), Guillermo Cabrera Infante (Cuba), Carlos Fuentes (Mexico), Jorge Edwards (Chile), Mario Vargas Llosa (Peru).

27. Lawaetz, Gudie, ed. and intro. *Spanish short stories: 2. Cuentos hispánicos: 2.* Harmondsworth & Baltimore: Penguin, 1972. 214 p. paper.

A bilingual edition, parallel texts.

Companion volume to No. 24, with more selections from the most outstanding contemporary writers.

Of 8 writers, 7 are Latin Americans. Includes representative stories by: Jorge Edwards (Chile), Mario Vargas Llosa (Peru), Juan Carlos Onetti (Uruguay), Carlos Fuentes (Mexico), Norberto Fuentes

(Cuba), Gabriel García Márquez (Colombia), Julio Cortázar (Argentina).

28. Levine, Suzanne Jill and Hallie D. Taylor, tr. *Triple Cross: Three short novels.* New York: E. P. Dutton, 1972. 329 p.

Works by three of the most important and innovative writers of contemporary Latin America: Carlos Fuentes (Mexico), *Holy Place* (*Zona sagrada,* 1967); José Donoso (Chile), *Hell has no limits* (*El lugar sin límites,* 1966); Severo Sarduy (Cuba), *From Cuba with a song* (*De donde son los cantantes,* 1967).

This collection is an important addition to the bibliography of Latin American fiction in English translation.

29. Mancini, Pat McNees, ed. and intro. *Contemporary Latin American short stories.* Greenwich, Connecticut: Fawcett, 1974. 479 p. bibliog. paper.

Various translators. Good selections of twentieth-century literature by recognized translators. Includes notes on authors and a bibliography (pp. 475-479).

Spanish American writers are: Rubén Darío (Nicaragua), Leopoldo Lugones (Argentina), Horacio Quiroga (Uruguay), Rómulo Gallegos (Venezuela), Miguel Angel Asturias (Guatemala), Jorge Icaza (Ecuador), Juan Bosch (Dominican Republic), Roberto Arlt (Argentina), Jorge Luis Borges (Argentina), Alejo Carpentier (Cuba), Octavio Paz (Mexico), Julio Cortázar (Argentina), Juan José Arreola (Mexico), Augusto Roa Bastos (Paraguay), Hernando Téllez (Colombia), Adolfo Bioy

Casares (Argentina), María Luisa Bombal (Chile), Juan Rulfo (Mexico), Carlos Fuentes (Mexico), Gabriel García Márquez (Colombia), José Donoso (Chile), René Marqués (Puerto Rico), Juan Carlos Onetti (Uruguay), Mario Benedetti (Uruguay), Pedro Juan Soto (Puerto Rico), Guillermo Cabrera Infante (Cuba), Norberto Fuentes (Cuba), Mario Vargas Llosa (Peru), Manuel Puig (Argentina), Abelardo Castillo (Argentina), José Agustín (Mexico).

For Brazilian writers see No. 424.

30. Moore, Evelyn, ed. and tr. *Sancocho; stories and sketches of Panama.* Panama: Panama American Publishing Co., 1938. 194 p.

The most extensive (although dated) source of Panamanian short fiction.

Selections by: Guillermo Andreve, Julio Arjona, Lucas Bárcena, M. Francisco Carrasco, R. E. J. Castilleros, Moisés Castillo, Elida L. C. de Crespo, José Huerta, Samuel Lewis, Santiago McKay ("Fray Rodrigo"), Octavio Méndez Pereira, Salomón Ponce Aguilera, Graciela Rojas Sucre, Nacho Valdés.

31. Onís, Harriet ed, ed. *Spanish stories and tales.* New York: Knopf, 1954. 270 p. (rpt. New York: Washington Square Pr., 1968. paper) *

The anthology also includes stories by Spanish writers. Various translators.

Selections are uneven in quality, featuring works from the first half of the twentieth century.

Spanish American authors are: Jorge Luis Borges (Argentina), Arturo Cancela (Argentina), Rómulo Gallegos (Venezuela), Ricardo Güiraldes (Argentina), Eduardo Mallea (Argentina), Lino Novás Calvo (Cuba), Ricardo Palma (Peru), Horacio Quiroga (Uruguay), Arturo Souto Alabarce (Mexico), Benjamín Subercaseaux (Chile), Hernando Téllez (Colombia), Carlos Wyld Ospina (Guatemala).

32. *Prize stories from Latin America: Winners of the 'Life en Español' literary contest.* Pref. Arturo Uslar Pietri. Garden City, N.Y.: Doubleday, 1963. 398 p. (rpt. 1964. 383 p. paper) *

A translation by various translators of *Ceremonia secreta y otros cuentos de América Latina premiados en el Concurso Literario de 'Life en Español', 1960, 1961.*
An interesting work which collects the literary production of mostly young and inexperienced writers.
The collection includes "Secret ceremony," by Marco Denevi (Argentina), the first-prize winner.
Other writers are: Carlos Martínez Moreno (Uruguay), Alfonso Echeverría (Chile), Tomás Mojarro (Mexico), Laura del Castillo (Argentina), Faustino González Aller (Cuba), Carlos Rozas Larraín (Chile), Haroldo Pedro Conti (Argentina), Juan Carlos Onetti (Uruguay), Ramón Ferreira López (Cuba), Rolando Venturini (Argentina).

33. *Spanish stories: Cuentos españoles; stories in the original Spanish, with new English translations.* New York: Bantam, 1960. xii, 339 p. paper (London: Bantam, 1961)

Stories by Spanish and Spanish American writers. Anonymous translations. A bilingual edition.
Latin American selections are by three highly regarded prose writers of the first part of the twentieth century [Benito Lynch (Argentina), Ricardo Palma (Peru), Horacio Quiroga (Uruguay)] and world renowned Jorge Luis Borges (Argentina).

34. Starr, Frederick, ed. and tr. *Readings from modern Mexican authors.* Chicago: Open Court, 1904. xii, 420 p.* (London: Kegan Paul, Trench, Trubner, 1904).

Excerpts, with biographical notes, from works by 29 Mexican authors, from the colonial period to nineteenth-century romantics, naturalists, and realists. They include: Luis González Obregón, Ignacio M. Altamirano, José López Portillo y Rojas, Rafael Delgado, Federico Gamboa, and others.

35. Torres-Rioseco, Arturo, ed. *Short stories of Latin America.* Tr. Zoila Nelken and Rosalie Torres-Rioseco. New York: Las Americas, 1963, 203 p.*

Selected works by widely read contemporary prose writers.
Stories by: Félix Pita Rodríguez (Cuba), Lino Novás Calvo (Cuba), Andrés Henestrosa (Mexico), Alejo Carpentier (Cuba), Guadalupe Dueñas (Mexico), Alfredo Pareja Diez-Canseco (Ecuador), Juan Marín (Chile), Jorge Luis Borges (Argentina), Horacio Quiroga (Uruguay), María Luisa Bombal (Chile), Ciro Alegría (Peru), Manuel Rojas (Chile), Agustín Yáñez (Mexico).
A story by exiled Spanish writer Francisco Ayala is also included.

36. Yates, Donald, ed. *Latin blood; the best crime and detective stories of South America*. Tr. and intro. Donald A. Yates, Isabel Reade, and Michael G. Gafner. New York: Herder and Herder, 1972. xv, 224 p.

A most interesting and valuable addition to the growing number of Latin American anthologies in English translation. The only collection of its kind.

Stories by: Alberto Edwards (Chile), Jorge Luis Borges (Argentina) (2), Manuel Peyrou (Argentina), Rodolfo J. Walsh (Argentina) (2), Velmiro Ayala Gauna (Argentina), H. Bustos Domecq [Jorge Luis Borges and Adolfo Bioy Casares] (Argentina), Antonio Helú (Mexico), María Elvira Bermúdez (Mexico), Dalmiro A. Sáenz (Argentina), Alfonso Ferrari Amores (Argentina), L. A. Isla (Chile), Hernando Téllez (Colombia), Enrique Anderson Imbert (Argentina), Pepe Martínez de la Vega (Mexico), W. I. Eisen [Isaac Eisenberg] (Argentina).

3. Poetry

37. Ahern, Maureen and David Tipton, ed. and tr. *Peru: The new poetry*. London: London Magazines Editions, 1970. 128 p.

Translations of 12 contemporary poets, with emphasis on the works of Carlos Germán Belli and Antonio Cisneros. The edition includes a short intro. by Tipton, prose statements (by Antonio Cisneros, Rodolfo Hinostrosa, Wáshington Delgado, and Sebastián Salazar Bondy) about the poetic climate of Peru, and biographical notes.

Poets: Sebastián Salazar Bondy, Francisco Carrillo, Wáshington Delgado, Carlos Germán Belli, Juan Gonzalo Rose, Pablo Guevara, Rodolfo Hinostrosa, Antonio Cisneros, Javier Heraud, Marco Martos, Julio Ortega, Mirko Lauer.

38. Amy, Francisco Javier, ed. and tr. *Musa bilingüe; being a collection of translation, principally from the standard Anglo-Amiercan poets, into Spanish; and Spanish, Cuban and Porto Rican poets into English, with the original text opposite, and biographical notes; especially intended for the use of students*. Tr. Francisco Javier Amy, William Cullen Bryant, and L. E. Levy. San Juan, Puerto Rico: Press of "El Boletín Mercantil," 1903. 329 p.

Poems by minor nineteenth-century poets. Of little interest today.

Spanish Americans included are: Francisco Javier Amy (Puerto Rico), José Gautier Benítez (Puerto Rico), José María Heredia (Cuba), Rafael María de Mendive (Cuba), José Jacinto Milanés y Fuentes (Cuba), Francisco Sellén (Cuba), Juan Clemente Zenea (Cuba).

39. [Beck, Claudia] and [Sylvia Carranza], ed. *Cuban poetry, 1959-1966*. Foreword Heberto Padilla and Luis Suardíaz. Havana: Book Institute, 1967. 788 p.

A bilingual edition. Various translators. Poets chosen for inclusion in the collection have published at least one book of poems. There are from 2 to 12 selections by each poet.

Poems by: Manuel Navarro Luna, Nicolás Guillén, Félix Pita Rodríguez, Angel Augier, Adolfo Menéndez Alberdi, José Lezama Lima, Samuel Feijóo, Aldo Menéndez, Oscar Hurtado, Alcides Iznaga,

Eliseo Diego, Cintio Vitier, Jesús Orta Ruiz (Indio Naborí), Rolando Escadró, Luis Marré, Francisco de Oraá, Roberto Branly, Roberto Fernández Retamar, Pablo Armando Fernández, Fayad Jamís, José Martínez Matos, Luis Pavón, Pedro de Oraá, José Alvarez Baragaño, Heberto Padilla, Rafael Alcides, César López, Raúl Luis, Domingo Alfonso, Antón Arrufat, Manuel Díaz Martínez, Luis Suardíaz, Armando Alvarez Bravo, Joaquín González Santana, Miguel Barnet, David Fernández, Belkis Cuza Malé, Guillermo Rodríguez Rivera, Víctor Casaus, Nancy Morejón.

40. Benedetti, Mario, ed. and intro. *Unstill life. Naturaleza viva: An introduction to the Spanish poetry of Latin America.* Tr. Claribel Alegría and Darwin J. Flakoll. New York: Harcourt, Brace and World, 1969. 127 p. illus.

An attractively illustrated introductory text. Bilingual edition, parallel texts. Brief biobibliographical notes are included. One poem for each of 23 poets, from the modernist period to recent times.

The poets include: Rubén Darío (Nicaragua), Baldomero Fernández Moreno (Argentina), Gabriela Mistral (Chile), Alfonsina Storni (Argentina), César Vallejo (Peru), Vicente Huidobro (Chile), Juana de Ibarbourou (Uruguay), Nicolás Guillén (Cuba), Pablo Neruda (Chile), Juan Cunha (Uruguay), Octavio Paz (Mexico), Nicanor Parra (Chile), Joaquín Pasos (Nicaragua), Idea Vilariño (Uruguay), Sebastián Salazar Bondy (Peru), Claribel Alegría (El Salvador), Ernesto Cardenal (Nicaragua), Jaime Sabines (Mexico), Jorge Enrique Adorim

(Ecuador), Carlos Germán Belli (Peru), Roberto Fernández Retamar (Cuba), Juan Gelman (Argentina), Marco Antonio Montes de Oca (Mexico).

41. Benson, Rachel, ed. and tr. *Nine Latin American poets.* New York: Las Americas, 1968. 359 p. *

A bilingual edition, parallel texts, of poems by leading twentieth-century poets.

The nine poets are: José Gorostiza (Mexico), Vicente Huidobro (Chile), Pablo Neruda (Chile), Luis Palés Matos (Puerto Rico), Octavio Paz (Mexico), Carlos Pellicer (Mexico), Alfonsina Storni (Argentina), César Vallejo (Peru), Xavier Villaurrutia (Mexico).

42. Braymer, Nan and Lillian Lowenfels, tr. *Modern poetry from Spain and Latin America.* New York: Corinth Books, 1964. 63 p. *

Most of the poets are Spanish. The Spanish American poets are: Nicolás Guillén (Cuba), Agustín Millares (Mexico), Salomón de la Selva (Nicaragua), and César Vallejo (Peru).

43. Brotherston, Gordon and Edward Dorn, [ed.] and tr. *Our word: Guerilla poems from Latin America. Palabra del guerrillero: Poesía guerrillera de Latinoamérica.* London: Cape Goliard, 1968. 1 vol. unpaged [58 p.] (New York: Grossman, 1968)

Bilingual edition, parallel texts. Brief notes about the poets. Poems by and about guerillas, most of them published for the first time. Uneven literary quality.

Poems (total of 24) by: Ernesto Che Guevara (Argentina, Cuba), Luis de la Puente (Peru), Luis Nieto (Peru), Javier Heraud (Peru), Otto René Castillo (Guatemala), Marco Antonio Flores (Guatemala), Fernando Gordillo Cervantes (Nicaragua), Michele Najlis (Nicaragua), Pablo Hernando Guerrero (Cuba).

44. Caracciolo-Trejo, Enrique, ed. *The Penguin book of Latin American verse.* Intro. Henry Gifford. Harmondsworth & Baltimore: Penguin, 1971. xlv, 424 p. Indexes, paper

A comprehensive selection of poems from the colonial period to modern times. A good panorama of Latin American poetry.

Plain prose translations by various translators. Introductory essay, pp. xxxvii-xlv. This volume also includes an appendix, "An explanatory guide to movements in Latin-American poetry" (pp. 395-409).

Selections arranged alphabetically by country.

Argentina: Esteban Echeverría, José Hernández, Leopoldo Lugones, Baldomero Fernández Moreno, Enrique Banchs, Oliverio Girondo, Ezequiel Martínez Estrada, Ricardo E. Molinari, Jorge Luis Borges, Enrique Molina, Edgar Bayley, Alberto Girri, Raúl Gustavo Aguirre.

Bolivia: Ricardo Jaimes Freyre.

Brazil: See No. 427.

Chile: Vicente Huidobro, Gabriela Mistral, Pablo Neruda, Nicanor Parra, Enrique Lihn.

Colombia: Gregorio Gutiérrez González, José Asunción Silva, Guillermo Valencia, Porfirio Barba Jacob, León de Greiff, Alvaro Mutis.

Cuba: José Martí, Julián del Casal, Nicolás Guillén, Eugenio Florit, Emilio Ballagas, José Lezama Lima, Roberto Fernández Retamar, Pablo Armando Fernández.

Ecuador: José Joaquín de Olmedo, Jorge Carrera Andrade.

Guatemala: Luis Cardoza y Aragón.

Mexico: Salvador Díaz Mirón, Manuel José Othón, Manuel Gutiérrez Nájera, Enrique González Martínez, José Juan Tablada, Ramón López Velarde, Alfonso Reyes, Carlos Pellicer, José Gorostiza, Xavier Villaurrutia, Salvador Novo, Octavio Paz, Jaime Sabines, Marco Antonio Montes de Oca, José Emilio Pacheco.

Nicaragua: Rubén Darío, Ernesto Cardenal.

Peru: Manuel González Prada, José Santos Chocano, José María Eguren, César Vallejo, Martín Adán, Carlos Germán Belli.

Puerto Rico: Luis Lloréns Torres, Luis Palés Matos.

Uruguay: Julio Herrera y Reissig, Emilio Frugoni, Delmira Agustini, Carlos Sabat Ercasty, Emilio Oribe, Idea Vilariño.

Venezuela: Andrés Bello, Andrés Eloy Blanco, Rafael Cadenas.

45. Cohen, J[ohn] M[ichael], ed. and tr. *The Penguin book of Spanish verse.* Harmondsworth & Baltimore: Penguin, 1956. 441 p. paper

A bilingual edition with plain prose translations. Superseded by No. 44 as far as Latin American poetry is concerned. The majority of poets represented are Spanish.

Spanish American poets included are: Jorge Carrera Andrade (Ecuador), Alí Chumacero (Mexico), Rubén Darío (Nicaragua), Salvador Díaz Mirón (Mexico), Enrique González Martínez (Mexico), Nicolás

Guillén (Cuba), Julio Herrera y Reissig (Uruguay), Sor Juana Inés de la Cruz (Mexico), Ramón López Velarde (Mexico), Ricardo E. Molinari (Argentina), Pablo Neruda (Chile), Salvador Novo (Mexico), Silvina Ocampo (Argentina), Manuel José Othón (Mexico), Octavio Paz (Mexico),Alberto Quintero Alvarez (Mexico), Alfonso Reyes (Mexico), César Vallejo (Peru), Xavier Villaurrutia (Mexico).

46. Craig, George Dundas, comp. and tr. *The modernist trend in Spanish American poetry; a collection of representative poems of the modernist movement and the reaction, translated into English verse, with a commentary.* Berkeley: Univ. of California Pr., 1934, xii, 347 p. bibliog. (rpt. New York: Gordian Pr., 1971)

A bilingual edition, parallel texts. Used as a textbook at the university level for many years.

Poets included are: Enrique Banchs (Argentina), Jorge Luis Borges (Argentina) José Santos Chocano (Peru), Rubén Darío (Nicaragua), Enrique González Martínez (Mexico), Juan Guzmán Cruchaga (Chile), Julio Herrera y Reissig (Uruguay), Vicente Huidobro (Chile), Ricardo Jaimes Freyre (Bolivia), Leopoldo Lugones (Argentina), Gabriela Mistral (Chile), Pablo Neruda (Chile), Amado Nervo (Mexico), Carlos Pezoa Véliz (Chile), Pedro Prado (Chile), José Asunción Silva (Colombia), Víctor Domingo Silva (Chile), Alfonsina Storni (Argentina), Arturo Torres-Rioseco (Chile), Guillermo Valencia (Colombia).

47. Edwards, Agustín, ed. *My native*

land. London: Ernest Benne, 1929. 430 p.

Contains a collection of Chilean poetry in translation.

Poets included are: Julio Vicuña Cifuentes, Carlos Pezoa Véliz, Luis F. Contardo, D. Dublé Urrutia, Manuel Magallanes Moure, Francisco Contreras, Víctor Domingo Silva, Gabriela Mistral.

48. Fife, Austin E., ed. and tr. *Latin American interlude.* Logan, Utah: Utah State Univ. Pr., 1966. 83 p.*

A bilingual selection of poems, "Hispanic-American lyrics" (pp. 21-69) is included.

Selections of uneven quality by nineteenth and early twentieth-century poets. One or two poems by each poet.

Poets are: José Joaquín Pesado (Mexico), Joaquín Arcadio Pagaza (Mexico), José María Bustillos (Mexico), Rafael Obligado (Argentina), Luis G. Urbina (Mexico), Alfonsina Storni (Argentina), Rubén Darío (Nicaragua), Luis Carlos López (Colombia), Luis L. Franco (Argentina), Gabriela Mistral (Chile).

49. Fitts, Dudley, ed. *Anthology of contemporary Latin American poetry. Antologia de la poesia americana contemporánea.* Norfolk, Conn.: New Directions, 1942. 667 p. *

A bilingual edition. The anthology includes poems by seven Brazilian poets and three from Haiti.

The most comprehensive collection of Latin American poetry at the date of publication. Includes a wide selection of poems which reflects the production of the period. Many of the poets have been forgotten today.

Spanish American poets included are: Xavier Abril (Peru), Martín Adán (Peru), Eduardo Anguita (Chile), Rafael Arévalo Martínez (Guatemala), Rafael Alberto Arrieta (Argentina), Miguel Angel Asturias (Guatemala), Yolanda Bedregal de Cónitzer (Bolivia), Jorge Luis Borges (Argentina), Enrique Bustamente y Ballivián (Peru), Luis Cané (Argentina), Wilberto L. Cantón (Mexico), Luis Cardoza y Aragón (Guatemala), Eduardo Carranza (Colombia), Jorge Carrera Andrade (Ecuador), Alejandro Carrión (Ecuador), Oscar Castro Z. (Chile), Otto D'Sola (Venezuela), José María Eguren (Peru), Gonzalo Escudero (Ecuador), Genaro Estrada (Mexico), Rafael Estrada (Costa Rica), José Miguel Ferrer (Venezuela), Eugenio Florit (Cuba), Jacinto Fombona Pachano (Venezuela), Carmen Alicia Cadilla (Puerto Rico), Luis L. Franco (Argentina), Oliverio Girondo (Argentina), Gilberto González y Contreras (El Salvador), Enrique González Martínez (Mexico), José Gorostiza (Mexico), Nicolás Guillén (Cuba), Alfonso Gutiérrez Hermosillo (Mexico), José Ramón Heredia (Venezuela), Demetrio Herrera S. (Panama), Efraín Huerta (Mexico), Vicente Huidobro (Chile), Roberto Ibáñez (Uruguay), Juana de Ibarbourou (Uruguay), Claudia Lars (El Salvador), José Lezama Lima (Cuba), Luis Carlos López (Colombia), Francisco López Merino (Argentina), Leopoldo Marechal (Argentina), Rafael Maya (Colombia), Francisco Méndez (Nicaragua), Rafael Méndez Dorich (Peru), Gabriela Mistral (Chile), Manuel Moreno Jimeno (Peru), César Moro (Peru), Manuel Muñoz Marín (Puerto Rico), Conrado Nalé Roxlo (Argentina), Pablo Neruda (Chile), Salvador Novo (Mexico), Silvina Ocampo (Argentina), R. Olivares Figueroa (Venezuela), Carlos Oquendo de Amat (Peru), Emilio Oribe (Uruguay), Bernardo Ortiz de Montellano (Mexico), Raúl Otero Reiche (Bolivia), Miguel Otero Silva (Venezuela), Luis Palés Matos (Puerto Rico), Germán Pardo García (Colombia), Octavio Paz (Mexico), Regino Pedroso (Cuba), Carlos Pellicer (Mexico), Enrique Peña Barrenechea (Peru), Alejandro Peralta (Peru), Ildefonso Pereda Valdés (Uruguay), Angel Miguel Queremel (Venezuela), Alfonso Reyes (Mexico), Pablo de Rokha (Chile), Winett de Rokha (Chile), Hipólito Sánchez Quell (Paraguay), Salomón de la Selva (Nicaragua), Alfonsina Storni (Argentina), Constantino Suasnavar (Honduras), César Tiempo (Argentina), Jaime Torres Bodet (Mexico), Rafael Heliodoro Valle (Honduras), César Vallejo (Peru), José Varallanos (Peru), Emilio Vásquez (Peru), Pedro Juan Vignale (Argentina), Xavier Villaurrutia (Mexico), Emilio Adolfo von Westphalen (Peru), Luis Fabio Xammar (Peru).

50. Gannon, Patricio and Hugo Manning. *Argentine anthology of modern verse.* Pref. Patricio Gannon. Buenos Aires: Francisco A. Columbo, 1942. 73 p.

Poems of the early and mid-century.

Poems by: Rafael Alberto Arrieta, Enrique Banchs, Francisco Luis Bernárdez, Jorge Luis Borges, Baldomero Fernández Moreno, Eduardo González Lanuza, Enrique Larreta, Roberto Ledesma, Leopoldo Lugones, Leopoldo Marechal, Ricardo E. Molinari, Conrado Nalé Roxlo, Pedro Miguel Obligado, José Pedroni, Alfonsina Storni.

51. Goldberg, Issac, ed. *Mexican poetry; an anthology.* Girard, Kansas: Haldeman-Julius, 1925. 64 p. (Little Blue Book No. 810) *

A brief selection of poems by poets from colonial times to the post-modernists.

Poets are: Manuel Acuña, Rafael Cabrera, María Enriqueta Camarillo y Roa, Agustín F. Cuenca, Balbino Dávalos, Salvador Díaz Mirón, Enrique Fernández Granados, Manuel M. Flores, Enrique González Martínez, Manuel Gutiérrez Nájera, Sor Juana Inés de la Cruz, Amado Nervo, Manuel José Othón, José M. Pino, José Rosas Moreno, José Juan Tablada, Luis G. Urbina, Jesús E. Valenzuela.

52. _____. ed. and intro. *Some Spanish American poets.* Tr. Alice Stone Blackwell. New York & London: D. Appleton, 1929. xli, 559 p. (rpt. Philadelphia: Univ. of Pennsylvania Pr., 1937; rpt. London: H. Milford, Oxford Univ. Pr., 1937; rpt. New York: Greenwood Pr., 1968; rpt. New York: Biblo and Tannen, 1968)

A bilingual edition which includes notes and introductory material in Spanish and English.

One of the earliest comprehensive anthologies which contains work by long forgotten poets. Provides a panorama of the poetry from the colonial period to the post-modernists, with emphasis on nineteenth and early twentieth-century poets.

The poets are: Manuel Acuña, (Mexico), Almafuerte (Argentina), Enrique Alvarez Henao (Colombia), Olegario Víctor Andrade (Argentina), Rafael Arévalo Martínez (Guatemala), Santiago Argüello (Nicaragua), Andrés Bello (Venezuela), Rufino Blanco Fombona (Venezuela), Dulce María Borrero de Luján (Cuba), Mario Bravo (Argentina), Roberto Brenes Mesén (Costa Rica), Bonifacio Byrne (Cuba), Rafael Cabrera (Mexico), José A. Calcaño (Venezuela), José Eusebio Caro (Colombia), Joaquín Castellanos (Argentina), José Santos Chocano (Peru), Luis F. Contardo (Chile), Francisco Contreras (Chile), Agustín F. Cuenca (Mexico), Rubén Darío (Nicaragua), Balbino Dávalos (Mexico), Juan B. Delgado (Mexico), Salvador Díaz Mirón (Mexico), Luis L. Domínguez (Argentina), Manuel Duque (Bolivia), María Enriqueta Camarillo y Roa de Pereyra (Mexico), Demetrio Fábrega (Panama), Enrique Fernández Granados (Mexico), Fabio Fiallo (Dominican Republic), Julio Flores (Colombia), Manuel María Flores (Mexico), José Gautier Benítez (Puerto Rico), Alberto Ghiraldo (Argentina), Gertrudis Gómez de Avellaneda (Cuba), Alfredo Gómez Jaime (Colombia), Joaquín Gómez Vergara (Mexico, Jorge González B. (Chile), Enrique González Martínez (Mexico), Alejandro Guanes (Paraguay), Ricardo Gutiérrez (Argentina), Manuel Gutiérrez Nájera (Mexico), José María Heredia (Cuba), Julio Herrera y Reissig (Uruguay), David Hine (Costa Rica), Jorge Hübner (Chile), Juana de Ibarbourou (Uruguay), Francisco A. de Icaza (Mexico), Ricardo Jaimes Freyre (Bolivia), Sor Juana Inés de la

Cruz (Mexico), Leopoldo Lugones (Argentina), Luisa Luisi (Uruguay), M. Magallanes Moure (Chile), Mercedes Marín del Solar (Chile), Román Mayorga Rivas (El Salvador), Concha Meléndez (Puerto Rico), Gabriela Mistral (Chile), Bartolomé Mitre (Argentina), Amado Nervo (Mexico), Rafael Obligado (Argentina), José Joaquín de Olmedo (Ecuador), Luis G. Ortiz (Mexico), Manuel José Othón (Mexico), Benigno Palma (Panama), Ricardo Palma (Peru), Ramón de Palma y Romay (Cuba), Ignacio A. Pane (Paraguay), S. José M. Pino (Mexico), Rafael Pombo (Colombia), Pedro Prado (Chile), Carlos Augusto Salaverry (Peru), Justo Sierra (Mexico), José Asunción Silva (Colombia), Víctor Domingo Silva (Chile), Francisco Sosa (Mexico), Alfonsina Storni (Argentina), Jaime Torres Bodet (Mexico), Froylán Turcios (Honduras), Luis G. Urbina (Mexico), Salomé Ureña de Henríquez (Dominican Republic), Diego Uribe (Colombia), Guillermo Valencia (Colombia), Jesús E. Valenzuela (Mexico), José León del Valle (Mexico), Daniel de la Vega (Chile), Juan Zorrilla de San Martín (Uruguay).

53. Green, Ernest S. and Harriet von Lowenfels, ed. and tr. *Mexican and South American poems (Spanish and English).* San Diego, California: Dodge and Burbeck, 1892. 398 p. *

A collection of 19th-century Latin American poetry, also including selected works of Spaniard Núñez de Arce. Brief notes on each poet.

Among the many poets represented are: Manuel Acuña (Mexico), Gertrudis Gómez de Avellaneda (Cuba), Esteban Echeverría (Argentina), José María Heredia (Cuba), José Mármol (Argentina), and others.

54. Grucci, Joseph Leonard *et al,* tr. *Three Spanish American poets: Pellicer, Neruda, Andrade.* Albuquerque, N.M.: Swallow and Critchlow, 1942. 73 p.*

Poems by twentieth-century poets Carlos Pellicer (Mexico). tr. by Mary and C. V. Wicker; Pablo Neruda (Chile), by J. L. Grucci, and Jorge Carrera Andrade (Ecuador), by Lloyd Mallan.

55. Hays, H[offman] R[eynolds], ed., tr. and intro. *12 Spanish American poets; an anthology.* New Haven, Conn.: Yale Univ. Pr., 1943. 336 p. bibliog. (rpt. Boston: Beacon Pr., 1972)

A bilingual edition with notes about the poems and poets.

Poems by major poets with selections from the first half of the twentieth century.

The poets are: Jorge Luis Borges (Argentina), Jorge Carrera Andrade (Ecuador), Eugenio Florit (Cuba), Jacinto Fombona Pachano (Venezuela), José Gorostiza (Mexico), Nicolás Guillén (Cuba), Vicente Huidobro (Chile), Luis Carlos López (Colombia), Ramón López Velarde (Mexico), Pablo Neruda (Chile), Pablo de Rokha (Chile), César Vallejo (Peru).

56. Johnson, Mildred Edith, ed. and tr. *Swan, cygnets, and owl: An anthology of modernist poetry in Spanish America.* Intro. John S. Brushwood. Columbia: Univ. of Missouri Pr., 1956. 199 p.

A bilingual selection of poems written between 1885 and about 1956. Divided into three sections: "Precursors," "the Modernists," and "the Post-Modernists." Each section is preceded by short biographical sketches of the poets. Two to five poems for each poet.

Brushwood's essay, "An introductory essay on Modernism," is a full-length article (pp. 1-33).

Poets: Delmira Agustini (Uruguay), Rafael Arévalo Martínez (Guatemala), Rafael Alberto Arrieta (Argentina), Enrique Banchs (Argentina), Jorge Luis Borges (Argentina), Julián del Casal (Cuba), José Santos Chocano (Peru), Rubén Darío (Nicaragua), Enrique González Martínez (Mexico), Manuel González Prada (Peru), Manuel Gutiérrez Nájera (Mexico), Julio Herrera y Reissig (Uruguay), Juana de Ibarbourou (Uruguay), Ricardo Jaimes Freyre (Bolivia), Ramón López Velarde (Mexico), Leopoldo Lugones (Argentina), José Martí (Cuba), Pablo Neruda (Chile), Amado Nervo (Mexico), José Asunción Silva (Colombia), Alfonsina Storni (Argentina), Jaime Torres Bodet (Mexico).

57. Márquez, Robert, ed. and intro. *Latin American revolutionary poetry. Poesía revolucionaria latinoamericana.* New York & London: Monthly Review Pr., 1974. 505 p.

Bilingual edition, parallel texts. No more than 4 selections by any one poet. Various translators; however, most poems translated by the editor. Brief introductions for each poet. Some anonymous selections are included. Poets arranged by country.

The most serious and complete undertaking of its kind. An interesting social document as well as a panorama of socially and politically committed poetry.

Argentina: Enrique Molina, Juan Gelman, Víctor García Robles; Bolivia: Pedro Shimose; Brazil: Thiago de Mello; Chile: Enrique Lihn, (anonymous); Colombia: (anonymous); Cuba: Nicolás Guillén, Roberto Fernández Retamar, David Fernández Chericián, Nancy Morejón; Dominican Republic: Pedro Mir; Ecuador: Jorge Enrique Adorim; El Salvador: Roque Dalton; Guatemala: Otto René Castillo, Marco Antonio Flores; Haiti: René Depestre; Mexico: Juan Bañuelos; Nicaragua: Ernesto Cardenal, (anonymous); Peru: Antonio Cisneros, Arturo Corcuera, Javier Heraud; Puerto Rico: Pedro Pietri, Iván Silén, Iris M. Zavala; Uruguay: Mario Benedetti, Carlos María Gutiérrez; Venezuela: Edmundo Aray.

58. Matilla, Alfredo and Iván Silén, ed. and prol. *The Puerto Rican poets: Los poetas puertorriqueños.* New York: Bantam, 1972, xviii, 238 p. bibliog. paper

Bilingual edition, parallel texts. Includes twentieth-century poets, with special emphasis on the post-1950 generation in Puerto Rico and New York.

Poems by: Luis Lloréns Torres, Evaristo Ribera Chevremont, Juan Antonio Corretjer, Francisco Matos Paoli, Luis Palés Matos, Julia de Burgos, Hugo Margenat, José María Lima, Iris M. Zavala, Luis A. Rosario Quiles, Alfredo Matilla, Marina Arzola, Juan Sáez Burgos, Pedro Pietri, Jorge María Ruscalleda Bercedóniz, Angela María Dávila, Billy Cajigas, Iván Silén, Edwin Reyes Berríos, Angel Luis Méndez, Felipe Luciano, Víctor Hernández Cruz, Etnairis Rivera.

59. Patterson, Helen Wohl, comp. and tr. *Poetisas de América*. Prol. Jesús Flores Aguirre. Washington, D.C.: Mitchell Pr., 1960. 219 p. illus. paper *

Bilingual collection of translations and original poems in Spanish, English, French, and Portuguese. One to four selections by each poet. Poems by American poets are translated into Spanish. The anthology is the most extensive collection of works by women poets of Latin America. Arranged by country. Mostly twentieth century.

Argentina: María Paseyro, Alfonsina Storni; Bolivia: Yolanda Bedregal, María Quiroga Vargas, Lola Taborga de Requena; Brazil: Cecília Mereiles, Adalgisa Nery; Chile: Lucía Aguirre del Real, Gabriela Mistral; Colombia: Laura Victoria; Costa Rica: María Ester Amador, Ninfa Santos; Cuba: Gertrudis Gómez de Avellaneda, Dulce María Loynaz; Dominican Republic: Virginia Ortea; Ecuador: Rosa Borja de Ycaza, Dolores Veintemilla de Galindo; El Salvador: Claribel Alegría, Antonia Galindo, Claudia Lars; Guatemala: Romelia Alarcón Folgar, Margarita Carrera de Wever; Haiti: Marie-Thérèse Colimon, Emmeline Carriès Lemaire, Virginie Sampeur; Honduras: Fausta Ferrera; Mexico: Guadalupe Amor, María Enriqueta Camarillo, María del Mar, Margarita Paz Paredes, Sor Juana Inés de la Cruz, Rosario Sansores; Nicaragua: Amanda Aragón Somoza, Aura Rostand, María Teresa Sánchez; Panama: Esther María Osses, Matilde Real; Paraguay: Ida Talavera de Fracchia; Peru: Teresa María Llona, María Wiesse; Puerto Rico: María Cadilla de Martínez, Amelia Ceide, Providencia Rancho; Uruguay: Delmira Agustini, Juana de Ibarbourou, María Eugenia Vaz-Ferreira; Venezuela: Enriqueta Arvelo Larriva, Sor María Josefa de los Angeles.

Poems by the editor and two other women poets from the United States conclude the collection.

60. _____. comp. and tr. *Rubén Darío y Nicaragua: Bilingual anthology of poetry*. Washington, D.C.: American Literary Accents, 1966. 67 p. paper*

Includes examples of Darío's modernist poems and selections from twentieth-century Nicaraguan poetry.

Includes verse translations of the following poets: Rubén Darío (15 poems), Gilberto Barrios, Adolfo Calero-Orozco, Ernesto Cardenal, Alfonso Cortés, Pablo Antonio Cuadra, Julio Linares, Luis Mejía-González, María Theresa Sánchez, María de la Selva (Aura Rostand), Salomón de la Selva.

61. Paz, Octavio, ed. and intro. *Anthology of Mexican poetry*. Tr. Samuel Beckett. Pref. C. M. Bowra. Bloomington, Ind.: Indiana Univ. Pr., 1958. 213 p. (rpt. London: Thames and Hudson, 1959; London: Calder and Boyars, 1970. 213 p.)

This volume, one of the series of Representative Works of Latin American Literature of UNESCO, has enjoyed subsequent printings by Indiana Univ. Pr.

A collection of 100 poems by 35 poets, from the sixteenth to the twentieth century. No poetry from Indian languages nor examples of popular poetry (such as the *corridos*) is included. The work contains two long introductory essays by Bowra and

Paz, and biobibliographical notes on the poets (pp. 199-213).

Poets: Manuel Acuña, Juan Ruiz de Alarcón, Ignacio Manuel Altamirano, Bernardo de Balbuena, Matías de Bocanegra, Fernando de Córdova y Bocanegra, Salvador Díaz Mirón, Manuel M. Flores, Fernán González de Eslava, Francisco González León, Enrique González Martínez, Miguel de Guevara, Manuel Gutiérrez Nájera, Francisco A. de Icaza, Sor Juana Inés de la Cruz, Rafael López, Ramón López Velarde, José Manuel Martínez de Navarrete, Amado Nervo, Manuel José Othón, Joaquín Arcadio Pagaza, Manuel de la Parra, José Peón y Contreras, José Joaquín Pesado, Ignacio Ramírez, Efrén Rebolledo, Alfonso Reyes, Vicente Riva Palacio, Ignacio Rodríguez Galván, Luis de Sandoval y Zapata, Justo Sierra, Carlos de Sigüenza y Góngora, José Juan Tablada, Francisco de Terrazas, Luis G. Urbina.

62. Poor, Agnes Blake, comp. *Pan American poems; an anthology.* Tr. Agnes Blake Poor and William Cullen Bryant. Boston: The Gorham Pr., 1918. 80 p. *

Poems from the early nineteenth to the early twentieth century.

Spanish American poets are: Francisco Acuña de Figueroa (Uruguay), Juan Cruz Varela (Argentina), Agustín F. Cuenca (Mexico), Rubén Darío (Nicaragua), José de Diego (Puerto Rico), Esteban Echeverría (Argentina), Santiago Escuti Orrego (Chile), Arturo Giménez Pastor (Argentina), Gertrudis Gómez de Avellaneda (Cuba), José María Heredia (Cuba), Hermógenes Irisarri (Chile), D. A. Lozano (Venezuela), Manuel María Madiedo (Colombia),

Diego Maisias y Calle (Peru), José Mármol (Argentina), Pedro J. Naón (Argentina), José Joaquín de Olmedo (Ecuador), Mariano Ramallo (Bolivia), José Rivera Indarte (Argentina), Narciso Tondreau (Chile), Florencio Varela (Argentina), Domingo de Vivero (Peru), Ethelberto Zegarra Ballón (Peru), Juan Zorrilla de San Martín (Uruguay).

Brazilian poets included in the anthology are: Antonio Gônçalves Dias, Francisco Manuel, and Bruno Seabra.

63. Resnick, Seymour, comp. and pref. *Spanish American poetry; a bilingual selection.* Irvington-on-Hudson, N.Y.: Harvey House, 1964. 96 p. illus.

Various translators. Short selections, sometimes fragments of long poems. Some excerpts from the colonial period, but mostly from the nineteenth and early twentieth centuries.

Poets: Manuel Acuña (Mexico), José Eusebio Caro (Colombia), José Santos Chocano (Peru), Rubén Darío (Nicaragua), Luis L. Domínguez (Argentina), Alonso de Ercilla y Zúñiga (Chile), Fabio Fiallo (Dominican Republic), Gertrudis Gómez de Avellaneda (Cuba), Enrique González Martínez (Mexico), Manuel González Prada (Peru), Carlos Guido y Spano (Argentina), Manuel Gutiérrez Nájera (Mexico), José María Heredia (Cuba), Juana de Ibarbourou (Uruguay), Francisco Icaza (Mexico), Sor Juana Inés de la Cruz (Mexico), Leopoldo Lugones (Argentina), José Martí (Cuba), Mariano Melgar (Peru), Gabriela Mistral (Chile), Pablo Neruda

(Chile), Amado Nervo (Mexico), José Joaquín de Olmedo (Ecuador), Plácido (Cuba), José Asunción Silva (Colombia), Alfonsina Storni (Argentina), Juan del Valle y Caviedes (Peru).

63a. Ruiz del Vizo, Hortensia, ed. *Black poetry of the Americas (a bilingual anthology).* Miami: Ediciones Universal, 1972. 176 p. paper.

Provides a panoramic survey of the poetry of black writers from South America (including Jorge de Lima and Carlos Drummond de Andrade of Brazil) and the Caribbean. For poets whose native language is French, see No. 534. Emphasis is given to contemporary poets.

Selections by: Cuba: Felipe Pichardo Moya, Alfonso Camín, Ramón Guirao, Emilio Ballagas, Vicente Gómez Kemp, José Zacarías Tallet, Marcelino Arozarena, Alejo Carpentier, Regino Pedroso, Rafael Estenger, Nicolás Guillén, Félix B. Caignet, Francisco Vergara, José Sánchez-Boudy, Rolando Campíns, Jack Rojas, Ana Rosa Núñez, Alvaro de Villa, Armando Córdova, Anisia Meruelo González, Julio Hernández Miyares, Ana H. González.

From other countries; Luis Palés Matos (Puerto Rico), Candelario Obeso (Colombia), Hugo Salazar Valdés (Colombia), Jorge Artel (Colombia), Helcías Martán Góngora (Colombia), Juan Zapata Olivella (Colombia), Marco Fidel Chávez (Colombia), Irene Zapata Arias (Colombia), Manuel del Cabral (Dominican Republic), Demetrio Korsi (Panama), Andrés Eloy Blanco (Venezuela), Ildefonso Pereda Valdés (Uruguay).

64. Shand, William, ed. and tr. *Contemporary Argentine poetry.* Intro. Aldo Pellegrini. Buenos Aires: Fundación Argentina para la Poesía, 1969. xii, 275 p.

65. Strand, Mark, ed. *New poetry of Mexico: Selected with notes by Octavio Paz, Alí Chumacero, José Emilio Pacheco, and Homero Aridjis.* Intro. Octavio Paz. New York: E. P. Dutton, 1970. 224 p. index. * (rpt. London: Secker and Warburg, 1972. 187 p.)

Various translators. Less than one third of *Poesía en movimiento: México, 1915-1966* (1966). Reduced from 42 to 24 poets, and far fewer poems. Lesser poets and poems found to be difficult to translate well are not included. The intro. by Paz is a selection from a longer essay which serves as intro. to the original Mexican edition.

A bilingual text, parallel texts. Most poets represented by four to nine poems. Arranged chronologically.

Selections by: Homero Aridjis, José Emilio Pacheco, Oscar Oliva, Francisco Cervantes, Jaime Augusto Shelley, Sergio Mondragón, Gabriel Zaid, Marco Antonio Montes de Oca, Tomás Segovia, Jaime Sabines, Jaime García Terrés, Juan José Arreola, Alí Chumacero, Efraín Huerta, Octavio Paz, Gilberto Owen, Salvador Novo, Xavier Villaurrutia, José Gorostiza, Manuel Maples Arce, Carlos Pellicer, Julio Torri, Ramón López Velarde, José Juan Tablada.

66. Tarn, Nathaniel, ed. *Con Cuba; an anthology of Cuban poetry of the last sixty years.* London: Cape

Goliard Pr., 1969. 143 p. (New York: Grossman, 1969) *

A bilingual edition, parallel texts. Various translators.
A collection of twentieth-century poetry featuring the work of poets from post-1959 Cuba. Thirty poets represented.
Poets: Rafael Alcides, Orlando Alomá, Miguel Barnet, Víctor Casaus, Belkis Cuza Malé, Manuel Díaz Martínez, Eliseo Diego, Froilán Escobar, Samuel Feijóo, Lina de Feria, David Fernández, Pablo Armando Fernández, Roberto Fernández Retamar, Gerardo Fulleda León, Fina García Marruz, Félix Guerra, Fayad Jamís, José Lezama Lima, Eduardo Lolo, César López, Luis Marré, Nancy Morejón, Luis Rogelio Nogueras, Pedro de Oraá, Heberto Padilla, Félix Pita Rodríguez, Isel Rivero, Guillermo Rodríguez Rivera, Luis Suardíaz, Cintio Vitier.

67. Townsend, Francis Edward, ed., tr., and intro. *Quisqueya; a panoramic anthology of Dominican verse.* México: Editores Unidos, 1947. 104 p. (Rpt. Ciudad Trujillo: Editora del Caribe, 1954. 101 p.; rpt. as *Quisqueya; an English-Spanish version of the poetry of Santo Domingo.* Bogotá: UISIS, 1964. 63 p.)

The only comprehensive survey of the poetry of the Dominican Republic in English translation.
Poems by: Rafael Richiez Acevedo ("Agapito Javalera"), Enrique Aguiar, Osvaldo Bazil, Federico Bermúdez, Franklin Mieses Burgos, Manuel Cabral, Enrique Cambier, J. Agustín Concepción, Pedro René Contín Aybar, Gastón F. Deligne,

Vigil Díaz, Virgilio Díaz Ordóñez, Francisco Domínguez Charro, Alfredo Fernández Simo, Fabio Fiallo, Víctor Garrido, Valentia Giro, Clemencia Damirón Gómez P., Ernestina Gómez de Read, Miguel A. Guerrero, Enrique Henríquez, Gustavo Julio Henríquez, Rafael A. Henríquez, Tomás Hernández Franco, Porfirio Herrera, Héctor Incháustegui Cabral, Ramón Emilio Jiménez, Martha Lamarche, Julio de Windt Lavandier, Mariano Lebrón Saviñón, Tomás Morel, Domingo Moreno Jiménez, Amada Nivar de Pitaluga, Armando Oscar Pacheco, Arturo B. Pellerano Castro, Emilio Prudhomme, Rafael Emilio Sanabia, Altagracia Saviñón, Rubén Suro, Delia Weber.

68. *Translations from Hispanic poets.* New York: Hispanic Society of America, 1938. xvi, 271 p. *

Most of the poets are from the early twentieth century, including the most famous modernists and post-modernists.
Latin American poets included on pp. 183-265. They include: Enrique Banchs (Argentina), Andrés Bello (Venezuela), Oscar Bietti (Argentina), María Enriqueta Camarillo y Roa de Pereyra (Mexico), Julián del Casal (Cuba), José Santos Chocano (Peru), Sor Juana Inés de la Cruz (Mexico), Rubén Darío (Nicaragua), Salvador Díaz Mirón (Mexico), Gertrudis Gómez de Avellaneda (Cuba), Enrique González Martínez (Mexico), Manuel González Prada (Peru), Manuel Gutiérrez Nájera (Mexico), Juana de Ibarbourou (Uruguay), Francisco de Icaza (Mexico), Jorge Isaacs (Colombia), Martiniano Leguizamón (Argentina), Luis Carlos López (Colombia), Leopoldo

Lugones (Argentina), Fernando Luján (Costa Rica), José Julián Mariño (Cuba), Gabriela Mistral (Chile), Bartolomé Mitre (Argentina), Amado Nervo (Mexico), Emilio Oribe (Uruguay), Joaquín Arcadio Pagaza (Mexico), Carlos Pezoa Véliz (Chile), Carlos Luis Sáenz (Costa Rica), José Asunción Silva (Colombia), Alfonsina Storni (Argentina), Jaime Torres Bodet (Mexico).

69. Underwood, Edna Worthley, ed., tr. and intro. *Anthology of Mexican poets from the earliest times to the present day.* Portland, Maine: The Mosher Pr., 1932. xxxiii, 332 p. *

A comprehensive collection which includes many obscure poets.

Contents: 48 "poets of today," 40 "poets of yesterday," and 14 "prose miniatures."

Poets: Manuel Acuña, Juan Ruiz de Alarcón, Wenceslao Alpuche, Ignacio M. Altamirano, Ricardo Arenales, Roberto Argüellos Bringas, Carlos Barrera, José M. Bustillos, Fernando Calderón, María Enriqueta Camarillo y Roa de Pereyra, Rubén M. Campos, Manuel Carpio, Joaquín D. Casasús, E. A. Chávez, Eduardo Colin, Felipe T. Contreras, José Peón Contreras, Francisco G. Cosmes, Juan Díaz Covarrubias, Agustín F. Cuenca, Balbino Dávalos, Juan B. Delgado, Rafael Delgado, Manuel Díaz Mirón, Salvador Díaz Mirón, Genaro Estrada, José Joaquín Fernández de Lizardi, Enrique Fernández Granados, Manuel M. Flores, José D. Frías, F. González Guerrero, Enrique González Martínez, Enrique González Rojo, José Gorostiza, Manuel Gutiérrez Nájera, Francisco A. de Icaza, Luciano Joublanc Rivas, Sor Juana Inés de la Cruz, Manuel Larrañaga Portugal, Rafael López, Ramón López Velarde, Rafael Lozano, Jr., Ignacio M. Luchichi, Manuel V. Maples Arce, Ignacio Mariscal, Ignacio Martes de Oca, Miguel Gerónimo Martínez, Antonio Médiz Bolio, Francisco Monterde, Fray Manuel Navarrete, Amado Nervo, José J. Novelo, Salvador Novo, Francisco M. Olaguibel, Manuel Olaguibel, Bernardo Ortiz de Montellano, Manuel José Othón, Gilberto Owen, Joaquín Arcadio Pagaza, Manuel de la Parra, Carlos Pellicer, José Peón y Contreras, Pedro I. Pérez Piña, Juan de Dios Peza, Guillermo Prieto, Ignacio Ramírez, Efrén Rebolledo, Alfonso Reyes, Vicente Riva Palacio, José Pablo Rivas, José María Roa Bárcena, Luis Rosado Vega, José Rosas Moreno, Juan Manuel Ruiz Esparza, Franz Sáenz Azcorra, Justo Sierra, José Juan Tablada, Joaquín Téllez, Francisco de Terrazas, Jaime Torres Bodet, Pantaleón Tovar, Luis G. Urbina, Rodolfo Usigli, Jesús E. Valenzuela, Juan Valle, Xavier Villaurrutia, Rafael Enrique Zayos.

70. Walsh, Thomas, ed. *Hispanic anthology: Poems translated from the Spanish by English and North American poets.* New York & London: Putnam's, 1920. xii, 779 p. (rpt. Millwood, N.Y.: Kraus, 1969)

Translations by 18 translators in this bilingual edition. Included are biographical sketches of the poets.

Although the anthology contains selections from the colonial period, most of the poets are from the late nineteenth or early twentieth centuries.

The poets are: Olegario Víctor Andrade (Argentina), Rafael Arévalo Martínez (Guatemala), Rufino Blanco Fombona (Venezuela), Mariano

Brull (Cuba), José Eusebio Caro (Colombia), Ricardo Carrasquilla (Colombia), Julián del Casal (Cuba), José Santos Chocano (Peru), Luis Felipe Contardo (Chile), Rubén Darío (Nicaragua), Virgilio Dávila (Puerto Rico), Balbino Dávalos (Mexico), Salvador Díaz Mirón (Mexico), Alonso de Ercilla y Zúñiga (Chile), Fabio Fiallo (Dominican Republic), Julio Flores (Colombia), Gertrudis Gómez de Avellaneda (Cuba), Antonio Gómez Restrepo (Colombia), Enrique González Martínez (Mexico), Alfonso Guillén Zelaya (Honduras), Manuel Gutiérrez Nájera (Mexico), José María Heredia (Cuba), Enrique Hernández Miyares (Cuba), Julio Herrera y Reissig (Uruguay), Dimitri Ivanovitch (Colombia), Sor Juana Inés de la Cruz (Mexico), Samuel A. Lillo (Mexico), Muna Lee de Muñoz Marín (Puerto Rico), Luis C. López (Colombia), René López (Cuba), Leopoldo Lugones (Argentina), Manuel Magallanes Moure (Chile), Rafael María de Mendive (Cuba), Gabriela Mistral (Chile), Ernesto Montenegro (Chile), Luis Muñoz Rivera (Puerto Rico), Amado Nervo (Mexico), Luis G. Ortiz (Mexico), Joaquín Arcadio Pagaza (Mexico), Ricardo Palma (Peru), Felipe Pardo (Peru), Antonio Pérez-Pierret (Puerto Rico), Martina Pierra de Poo (Cuba), Ramón Pimentel Coronel (Venezuela), Rafael Pombo (Colombia), José Manuel Poveda (Cuba), Pedro Requena Legarreta (Mexico), Lola Rodríguez del Tió (Puerto Rico), José Rosas Moreno (Mexico), Antonio Sellén (Cuba), José Asunción Silva (Colombia), Víctor Domingo Silva (Chile), José Juan Tablada (Mexico), Diego Vicente Tejera (Cuba), Luis G. Urbina (Mexico), Guillermo Valencia (Colombia), José E. Valenzuela (Mexico), Daniel de la Vega (Chile), Juan José Velgas (Chile).

The collection also includes poems by Brazilians Bulhão Pato and Faqundes Varella.

71. *Young poetry of the Americas.* Vol. I. Washington, D.C.: Pan American Union, [196?]. 116 p.*

A bilingual collection of selections reprinted from issues of *Americas.* Various translators. Poems, with brief introductions, are arranged by country in short anthologies. They are:

"Seven Argentine poets" (ed. Manuel Grinberg and Juan Carlos Martelli): Alberto Cousté, Alejandro Vignati, Leopoldo José Bartolomé, Alejandra Pizarnik, Ignacio Beola, Marcelo Pichón Riviere, Juan Gelman;

"Five Chilean poets" (ed. José Donoso): Nicanor Parra, Efraín Barquero, Alberto Rubio, Enrique Lihn, Miguel Arteche;

"Eight Costa Rican poets": Jorge Debravo, Jorge Ibáñez, Laureano Albán, Julieta Doblez Yzaguirre, Marco Aguilar, Rodrigo Quirós, Alfonso Chase, Arabella Salaverry;

"Six Ecuadorian poets" (ed. Galo René Pérez and Ulises Estrella): Ana María Ixa, Francisco Araujo Sánchez, Manuel Zabala Ruiz, Carlos Manuel Arízaga, Euler Granda, Simón Corral;

"Four Salvadorian poets" (ed. Eunice Odio): Dora Guerra, Claudia Lars, Hugo Lindo, Pedro Geoffroy Rivas;

"Five Mexican poets" (ed. Sergio Mondragón): Octavio Paz, Joaquín Sánchez MacGregor, Homero Aridjis, José Emilio Pacheco, Jaime Augusto Shelley;

"Avant-garde poetry in Panama" (ed. Arístides Martínez Ortega): Carlos Francisco Chan-Marín, Tristán Solarte, Homero Icaza Sánchez, José de Jesús Martínez, Guillermo Ross Zanet, José Franco, Demetrio Fábrega;

"Six Uruguayan poets" (ed. Saúl Ibargoxen Islas): Mario Benedetti, Carlos Brandy, Juan Cunha, Milton Schinca, Jorge Medina Vidal, Idea Vilariño.

For Brazilian poets, see No. 435.
For Haitian poets, see No. 538.

4. Drama

72. Bierstadt, Edward Hale, ed. and intro. *Three plays of the Argentine.* Tr. Jacob S. Fassett. New York: Duffield, 1920. xlii, 148 p. *

Includes: Silverio Manco, *Juan Moreira* (*Juan Moreira*); Luis Bayón Herrera (born in Spain), *Santos Vega* (*Santos Vega,* 1913); Julio Sánchez Gardel, *The witches' mountain* (*La montaña de las brujas*, 1912).
Santos Vega is actually a dramatized poem based on the poetic character of Obligado. *Juan Moreira* is based on an earlier prose work of the same title.
Four appendices include notes, excerpts from the original Spanish versions of *Juan Moreira* and *Santos Vega,* and an essay by Spanish playwright Jacinto Benavente (pp. 142-147).

73. Colecchia, Francesca and Julio Matas, ed., tr. and intro. *Selected Latin American one-act plays.* Pittsburgh: Univ. of Pittsburgh Pr., 1973. xix, 204 p.

Works by 10 Spanish American dramatists from 7 countries. They include: Xavier Villaurrutia (Mexico),

Incredible though it seems (*Parece mentira,* 1934); Osvaldo Dragún (Argentina), *The man who turned into a dog* (from *Historias para ser contadas,* 1956); Elena Garro (Mexico), *A solid home* (*Un hogar sólido*, 1957); Carlos Solórzano (Guatemala), *Crossroads* (*Cruce de vías*, 1958); Gustavo Andrade Rivera (Colombia), *Remington 22* (*Remington 22,* 1961); Matías Montes Huidobro (Cuba), *The guillotine* (*La madre y la guillotina,* 1961); Luisa Josefina Hernández (Mexico), *Dialogues* (3 of 19 from *La calle de la gran ocasión,* 1961); Ramón Chalbaud (Venezuela), *The forceps* (*Las pinzas,* 1962), Julio Matas (Cuba), *Ladies at play* (*Juego de damas*); Jorge Díaz (Chile), *Love yourselves above all others* (*Amaos los unos sobre los otros* [originally *La pancarta*], 1971).

74. Jones, Willis Knapp, ed., tr. and intro. *Men and angels: Three South American comedies.* Carbondale, Illinois: Southern Illinois Univ. Pr., 1970. xlvi, 191 p. bibliog.

Includes the following works: Juan Fernando Camilo Darthés and Carlos S. Damel (Argentina), *The quack doctor* (*La hermana Josefina,* 1938); José María Rivarola Matto (Paraguay), *The fate of Chipi González* (*El fin de Chipí González,* 1954); Miguel Frank (Chile), *The man of the century* (*El hombre del siglo*, 1958).
The comedies are preceded by a long intro. (pp. xiii-xlvi) and the volume is completed by a "Checklist of translations of Latin American plays arranged alphabetically by countries and by names of dramatists" (pp. 181-191).

75. Luzuriaga, Gerardo and Robert

S. Rudder, ed., tr. and intro. *The orgy: Modern one-act plays from Latin America*. Los Angeles: UCLA Latin American Center, 1974. xxiii, 180 p. paper

A well-balanced collection of 11 works by established playwrights and lesser-known writers. The plays are:

Alberto Adellach (Argentina), *March (Marcha)* from *Homo dramaticus* (2nd ed., 1969); Enrique Buenaventura (Colombia), *The orgy (La orgía)* and *The schoolteacher (La maestra)* from *Los papeles del infierno* (1968); Marco Denevi (Argentina), *Romeo before the corpse of Juliet (Romeo frente al cadáver de Julieta)* and *You don't have to complicate happiness (No hay que complicar la felicidad)* from *Falsificaciones;* Jorge Díaz (Chile), *The eve of the execution, or Genesis was tomorrow (La víspera del degüello,* 1967); Osvaldo Dragún (Argentina), The story of Panchito González (Historia de Panchito González) and *The story of the man who turned into a dog (Historia del hombre que se convirtió en perro)* from *Historias para ser contadas* (1957); José Martínez Queirolo (Ecuador), *R. I. P. (Q. E. P. D.,* 1969); Alvaro Menén Desleal (pseud. of Alvaro Menéndez Leal) (El Salvador), *Black light (Luz negra,* 1966); Carlos Solórzano (Guatemala), *The crucifixion (El crucificado,* 1958).

76. Oliver, William I., ed., tr. and intro. *Voices of change in the Spanish American theater; an anthology.* Austin: Univ. of Texas Pr., 1971. xviii, 294 p.

Well chosen and translated plays, with an intro. on social conditions which influence contemporary Latin American dramatists.

Included are: Emilio Carballido (Mexico), *The day they let the lions loose (El día que se soltaron los leones,* 1957); Griselda Gambaro (Argentina), *The camp (El campo,* 1967); Carlos Maggi (Uruguay), *The library (La biblioteca,* 1959); Enrique Buenaventura (Colombia), *In the right hand of God the Father (En la diestra de Dios Padre,* 1960); Luisa Josefina Hernández (Mexico), *The mulatto's orgy* (1966); Sergio Vodánovic (Chile), *Viña: Three beach plays (Viña,* 1964).

77. *Plays of the southern Americas.* Stanford, California: Stanford Univ. Pr., 1942. 1 vol. unpaged [82 p.] (rpt. Freeport, N.Y.: Books for Libraries Pr., 1971)

The first of two volumes of translations which were published separately. For one-act plays, see No. 78.

Includes works by: Antonio Acevedo Hernández (Chile), *Cabrerita (Cabrerita),* tr. Wilbur E. Bailey; Florencio Sánchez (Uruguay), *The foreign girl (La gringa,* 1904), tr. Alfred Coester; Luis Vargas Tejada (Colombia), *My poor nerves (Las convulsiones),* tr. Wilbur E. Bailey.

78. *Short plays of the southern Americas.* Stanford, Cal.: Univ. Dramatists' Alliance, 1944. mimeo. *

Companion volume to *Plays of the southern Americas.* It includes the following selections: Florencio Sánchez (Uruguay), *Midsummer day parents (Cédulas de San Juan,* 1904); Pedro Pico (Argentina), *Common clay (Del mismo barro,* 1918); Eduardo Barrios (Chile), *For the sake of a good reputation (Por el decoro,* 1913); Jorge Zalamea (Colombia). *The inn of Bethlehem (El mesón de*

Belén, 1941); José Antonio Ramos (Cuba), *The traitor (El traidor);* Víctor Rendón (Ecuador), *The lottery ticket (Billete de lotería,* 1924); José Joaquín Gamboa (Mexico), *An old yarn (Cuento viejo,* 1930); Manuel Ascensio Segura (Peru), *Sergeant Canuto (El sargento Canuto*, 1839).

79. Woodyard, George, ed. and intro. *The modern stage in Latin America: Six plays; an anthology.* New York: E. P. Dutton, 1971. 331 p.

Various translators.

Five plays by Spanish Americans and one by a Brazilian dramatist. The Spanish Americans are: René Marqués (Puerto Rico), *The fanlights (Los soles truncos,* 1958); Osvaldo Dragún (Argentina), *And they told us we were immortal (Y nos dijeron que éramos inmortales*, 1963); Jorge Díaz (Chile), *The place where the mammals die (El lugar donde mueren los mamíferos*, 1963); José Triana (Cuba), *The criminals (La noche de los asesinos,* 1966); Emilio Carballido (Mexico), *I too speak of the rose (Yo también hablo de la rosa*, 1966).

The Brazilian work is by Alfredo Dias Gomes, *Payment as pledged (O pagador de promessas,* 1960).

This anthology includes representative selections of the most outstanding Latin American dramatists.

B. Individual Works

1. Novel

Argentina

80. Bioy Casares, Adolfo. *Diary of the War of the Pig.* Tr. Gregory

Woodruff and Donald A. Yates. New York: Herder and Herder, 1972. 196 p. (Subsequently distributed by McGraw-Hill [New York].)

(original title: *Diario de la guerra del cerdo,* 1969)
Novel that deals with the destructive tendency of mankind and its cruel disregard of the elderly.

81. Cortázar, Julio. *Hopscotch.* Tr. Gregory Rabassa. New York: Pantheon, 1966. 564 p. (London: Collins, Harvill Pr., 1967; rpt. New York: New American Library, 1969. 448 p. paper; rpt. New York: Avon, 1974. paper)

(original title: *Rayuela,* 1963)
Stylistically and thematically, one of the principal works of contemporary fiction. Set in Paris and Buenos Aires.

82. _____. *62: A model kit.* Tr. Gregory Rabassa. New York: Pantheon, 1972. 281 p. (rpt. New York: Avon, 1973. 288 p.)

(original title: *62: modelo para armar,* 1968)
A stylistically innovative view of contemporary society.

83. _____. *The winners.* Tr. Elaine Kerrigan. New York: Pantheon, 1965. 374 p. * (London: Souvenir Pr., 1965)

(original title: *Los premios,* 1960)
Brilliant study of characters from Buenos Aires; characterized by linguistic experimentation, humor, and symbolic meaning found in Cortázar's later novels.

84. Denevi, Marco. *Rosa at ten o'clock.* Tr. Donald A. Yates. New

York: Holt, Rinehart and Winston, 1964. 191 p. *

(original title: *Rosaura a las diez,* 1955)

Well-written murder mystery set in Buenos Aires.

85. Gálvez, Manuel. *Holy Wednesday.* Tr. Warre B. Wells. New York: Appleton, 1934. 208 p. * (London: John Lane, 1934. 169 p.)

(original title: *Miércoles santo*, 1930)

One of the important works of realist and social critic Gálvez.

86. _____. *Nacha Regules.* Tr. Leo Ongley. New York: Dutton, 1922. 304 p. * (London-Toronto: J. M. Dent and Sons, 1923)

(original title: *Nacha Regules*, 1919)

A priest defends a prostitute as he becomes himself a victim of social exploitation.

87. Guido, Beatriz. *End of a day.* Tr. A. D. Towers. New York: Scribner's, 1966. 278 p. *

(original title: *El incendio y las vísperas,* 1964)

Examines moral decay of the upper class under Peronism.

88. _____. *The house of the angel.* Tr. Joan Coyne MacLean. New York: McGraw-Hill, 1957. 172 p. * (London: Deutsch, 1958)

(original title: *La casa del ángel*, 1954)

A view of social pressure and intolerance achieved by the psychological study of a young adolescent girl.

89. Güiraldes, Ricardo. *Don Segundo Sombra; shadows on the pampas.* Tr. Harriet de Onís. New York: Farrar and Rinehart, 1935. 270 p.* (rpt. Harmondsworth, England: Penguin, 1948; rpt. New York: New American Library, 1966. illus. 222 p.*; rpt. London: New English Library, 1966)

(original title: *Don Segundo Sombra,* 1926)

The classic novel of the pampas, the stylized vision of the gaucho, and the character development of the boy who worships him.

90. Larreta, Enrique. *The glory of Don Ramiro; a life in the times of Philip II.* Tr. L. B. Walton. New York: Dutton, 1924. vii, 307 p.* (London-Toronto: Dent, 1924)

(original title: *La gloria de don Ramiro,* 1908)

An excellent historical novel and noteworthy example of Modernist prose in Latin America.

91. Mallea, Eduardo. *The bay of silence.* Tr. Stuart E. Grummon. New York: Knopf, 1944. 353 p.*

(original title: *La bahía del silencio*, 1940)

Deals with the frustrated search for meaning and personal authenticity in contemporary society.

92. _____. *Fiesta in November.* Tr. Alis de Sola. London: Calder and Boyars, 1969. 121 p.

(original title: *Fiesta en noviembre,* 1938)

First published in *All green shall perish, and other novellas and stories.* Ed. John B. Hughes. See No. 233.

Novel which gives a fictionalized account of the execution of Spanish poet Federico García Lorca, while stressing man's inability to communicate.

93. Mallea, Eduardo. *All green shall perish.* Tr. John B. Hughes. London: Calder and Boyars, 1967. 158 p.

(original title: *Todo verdor perecerá*, 1941)

First published in *All green shall perish, and other novellas and stories.* Ed. John B. Hughes. See No. 233.

A novel of alienation and lack of communication, and the anguish of life in a society without values.

94. Mármol, José. *Amalia; a romance of the Argentine.* Tr. Mary J. Serrano. New York: Dutton, 1919. xi, 419 p.* (rpt. 1944)*

(original title: *Amalia,* 1851-1855)

Romantic political novel of Buenos Aires during the regime of Argentine dictator Juan Manuel de Rosas.

95. Mujica Láinez, Manuel. *Bomarzo.* Tr. Gregory Rabassa. New York: Simon and Schuster, 1969. 573 p.* (London: Weidenfeld and Nicolson, 1970)

(original title: *Bomarzo,* 1962)

A fictionalized, sometimes fantastic biography of Duke Francesco Pier Orsini, an important figure of the Italian Renaissance.

96. Murena, H.A. [Héctor Alberto Alvarez]. *The laws of the night.* Tr. Rachel Caffyn. New York: Scribner's, 1970. 313 p.*

(original title: *Las leyes de la noche,* 1958)

Of a girl's anguish and alienation during the Perón era of Argentina. Murena reveals a very pessimistic view of man in a world without meaning.

97. Peyrou, Manuel. *Thunder of the roses; a detective novel.* Tr. Donald A. Yates. Intro. Jorge Luis Borges. New York: Herder and Herder, 1972. ix, 170 p.

(original title: *El estruendo de las rosas,* 1948)

Not merely a detective novel, among other things it analyzes the nature of dictatorship. Borges praises the novel in the introduction (pp. vii-ix).

98. Puig, Manuel. *Betrayed by Rita Hayworth.* Tr. Suzanne Jill Levine. New York: Dutton, 1971. 222 p. (rpt. New York: Avon, 1973. 254 p.)

(original title: *La traición de Rita Hayworth,* 1968)

A brilliant vision of provincial middle class society in which the language of the people is superbly recreated.

99. _____. *Heartbreak tango; a serial.* Tr. Suzanne Jill Levine. New York: Dutton, 1973. 224 p.

(original title: *Boquitas pintadas; folletín*, 1969)

As in *Betrayed by Rita Hayworth,* another view of society in provincial Argentina. Uses multiple points of view to present the frustrations and illusions of his characters.

100. Sábato, Ernesto. *The outsider.* Tr. Harriet de Onís. New York: Knopf, 1950. 177 p. *

(original title: *El túnel,* 1948)

An existentialist novel of considerable merit. Set in Buenos Aires.

101. West, Hugo [Gustavo A. Martínez Zuviría]. *Black Valley; a romance of the Argentine.* Tr. Herman and Miriam Hespelt. New York-London: Longmans, Green, 1928. 302 p.* (rpt. New York: Grosset, 1928)*

(original title: *Valle negro,* 1928)

Ignored by most literary critics, Wast's novels of sentimental love set in Buenos Aires and of country life have been immensely popular and widely translated.

102. _____. *The house of the ravens.* Tr. Leonard Matters. London: Williams and Norgate, 1924. 310 p.*

(original title: *La casa de los cuervos,* 1916)

103. _____. *Peach blossom.* Tr. Herman and Miriam Hespelt. New York-London: Longmans, Green, 1929. 300 p.*

(original title: *Flor de durazno,* 1911)

104. _____. *Stone desert.* Tr. Louis Imbert and Jacques Le Clercq. New York-London: Longmans, Green, 1928. 302 p.*

(original title: *El desierto de piedra,* 1925)

105. _____. *The strength of lovers.* Tr. Louis Imbert and Jacques Le Clercq. New York-London: Longmans, Green, 1930. 315 p. *

(original title: *Lucía Miranda,* 1930)

Bolivia

106. Costa du Rels, Adolfo. *Bewitched lands.* Tr. Stuart Edgar Grummon. New York: Knopf, 1945. 203 p.*

(original title: *Tierras hechizadas,* 1940)

Published originally in French (1931). Costa de Rels wrote many works in French as well as Spanish.

107. Prada [Oropeza], Renato. *The breach.* Tr. Walter Redmond. Garden City, N.Y.: Doubleday, 1971. 151 p.*

(original title: *Los fundadores del alba,* 1969)

Of revolutionaries in Bolivia. Prada is considered to be one of Bolivia's most promising young novelists.

Chile

108. Alegría, Fernando. *Lautaro.* Tr. Delia Goetz. New York: Farrar and Rinehart, 1944. 176 p.*

(original title: *Lautaro, joven libertador de Arauco,* 1943)

Fictionalized biography of the legendary Araucanian leader during the Spanish conquest of Chile.

109. _____. *My horse González.* Tr. Carlos Lozano. New York: Las Americas, 1964. 187 p. *

(original title: *Caballo de copas,* 1958)

Of experience of Latin Americans in San Francisco-Berkeley area, and marked cultural differences.

110. Barrios, Eduardo. *Brother*

Asno. Tr. Edmundo García Girón. New York: Las Americas, 1969. 134 p.*

(original title: *El hermano asno*, 1922)
Important psychological novel based on life in a monastery.

111. Blest Gana, Alberto. *Martín Rivas.* Tr. Mrs. Charles Whitham. New York: Alfred A. Knopf, 1918. 431 p.* (London: Chapman and Hall, 1916).

(original title: *Martín Rivas*, 1862)
A classic of the early stages of Latin American Realism depicting Chilean society during the middle part of the nineteenth century.

112. Bombal, María Luisa. *The house of mist.* Tr. and expanded by author. New York: Farrar-Straus, 1947. 245 p.* (Lòndon: Cassell, 1948. 184 p.)

(original title: *La última niebla*, 1935)
In a brief acknowledgement, the author gives credit to her husband (Fal de Saint Phalle) for his assistance in translating the work. The novel appears to have been simultaneously translated (from the title story of the collection *La última niebla*) and written in English (an expansion of that story). Highly lyrical prose which breaks with the *criollista* tradition in Chilean prose fiction.

113. _____. *The shrouded woman.* Tr. by the author. New York: Farrar-Straus, 1948, 198 p. *

(original title: *La amortajada*, 1938)
Subjective, psychological analysis of characters in the mind of a woman.

114. Coloane, Francisco. *The stowaway.* Tr. Adele Breaux. New York: Manyland Books, 1964. 113 p.

(original title: *El último grumete de 'La Baquedano',* 1941)
One of Coloane's several novels of the sea.

115. Donoso, José. *Coronation.* Tr. Jocasta Goodwin. New York: Knopf, 1965. 262 p.* (London: Bodley Head, 1965)

(original title: *Coronación*, 1957)
A penetrating vision of middle class society which examines at the psychological level the nature of reality and madness.

116. _____. *The obscene bird of the night.* Tr. Leonard Mades and Hardie St. Martin. New York: Knopf, 1973. 438 p. (London: Cape, 1974)

(original title: *El obsceno pájaro de la noche*, 1970)
This is a revised translation in English of the Spanish original.
A surrealistic novel of multiple points of view, striking imagery and fantastic events in the presentation of a family in disintegration.

117. _____. *This Sunday.* Tr. Lorraine O'Grady Freeman. New York: Knopf, 1967. 177 p. (London: Bodley Head, 1968)

(original title: *Este domingo,* 1965)
A more traditional novel of social relationships between the poor and the rich.

118. Huidobro, Vicente. *Mirror of a mage.* Tr. Warre B. Wells. Boston: Houghton-Mifflen, 1931. 185 p.* (London: Eyre and Spottiswoode, 1931)

(original title: *Cagliostro; novela-film,* 1926)

Experimental novel of Creationist poet Huidobro. Strong influence of the cinema in narrative techniques.

119. Huidobro, Vicente. *Portrait of a paladin.* Tr. Warre B. Wells. New York: Horace Liveright, 1932. 316 p.* (London: Eyre and Spottiswoode, 1932)

(original title: *Mío Cid campeador,* 1929)

A poet's version of the life of the Spanish epic hero.

120. Lafourcade, Enrique. *King Ahab's feast.* Tr. Renate and Ray Morrison. New York: St. Martin's Pr., 1963. 249 p.*

(original title: *La fiesta del rey Acab,* 1959)

A political novel about General Carrillo in Ciudad Carrillo, an obvious reference to strongman Trujillo of the Dominican Republic.

121. Martínez Bilbao, Oscar. *Hacienda.* Tr. Tita Caistor. Boston: Meador Publ. Co., (1960). 378 p.*

(original title unavailable)

Peasants are organized into unions and rebel against landowners. Representative of the politically motivated protest literature of scant (if any) literary value.

122. Petit Marfán, Magdalena. *La Quintrala.* Tr. Lulú Vargas Vila. New York: Macmillan, 1942. 190 p. *

(original title: *La Quintrala,* 1932)

Historical novel of the life of Doña Catalina de los Ríos, the "Lucrezia Borgia of Chile."

123. Prado, Pedro. *Country judge; a novel of Chile.* Tr. Lesley Byrd Simpson. Foreword Arturo Torres-Rioseco. Berkeley: Univ. of California Pr., 1968. xi, 143 p. (London: Cambridge Univ. Pr., 1967)

(original title: *Un juez rural,* 1924)

An idealized vision of life in a poor neighborhood.

124. Prieto, Jenaro. *The partner.* Tr. Blanca de Roig and Guy Dowler. London: Butterworth, 1931. 255 p.

(original title: *El socio,* 1928)

Novel of irony and satire of a businessman who invents a partner and must suffer the tragic consequences of his lie.

125. Rojas [Sepúlveda], Manuel. *Born guilty.* Tr. Frank Gaynor. New York: Library Publishers, 1955. 314 p.* (London: Gollancz, 1956)

(original title: *Hijo de ladrón,* 1951)

Novel of existentialist mode which serves as a landmark in Chilean fiction between *criollismo* and the modern novel.

126. Subercaseaux, Benjamín. *Jemmy Button.* Tr. Mary and Fred Villar. New York: Macmillan, 1954. x, 382 p.* (British edition edited and condensed by Oliver Coburn. London: W. H. Allen, 1955. 299 p.)

(original title: *Jemmy Button,* 1950)

Novel highlighted by philosophical reflections.

Colombia

127. García Márquez, Gabriel. *One hundred years of solitude.* Tr. Gregory Rabassa. New York: Harper and Row, 1970. 422 p. (London: Cape, 1970; rpt. New York: Avon, 1971. 383 p.; rpt. Harmondsworth, England: Penguin, 1972)

(original title: *Cien años de soledad*, 1967)

Traces several generations of the Buendía family in the mythical town of Macondo. A literary *tour de force* regarded by many to be the best novel of his generation, perhaps the most outstanding work of Latin American fiction.

128. Isaacs, Jorge. *María; a South American romance.* Tr. Rollo Ogden. Intro. Thomas A. Janvier. New York: Harper, 1890. xi, 302 p. (rpt. 1918, 1925)*

(original title: *María*, 1867)

Probably the most widely read novel of the Romantic movement in Latin American literature.

129. Marroquín, Lorenzo. *Pax (Peace).* Tr. Isaac Goldberg and Wolf von Schierbrand. Intro. Isaac Goldberg. New York: Brentano's, 1920. viii, 480 p.*

(original title: *Pax; novela de costumbres latino-americanas,* 1907)

José María Rivas Groot collaborated with Marroquín in this social novel of cultural conflict.

130. Rivera, José Eustasio. *The vortex.* Tr. Earle K. James. New York: Putnam, 1935. 320 p.*

(original title: *La vorágine*, 1924)

A couple flees to the jungle only to be transformed and eventually destroyed there. One of the most important novels of the period.

Costa Rica

131. Sánchez, José León. *God was looking the other way.* Anon. tr. Boston-Toronto: Little, Brown, 1973. 271 p.

(original title: *La isla de los hombres solos,* 1970)

Autobiographical novel written in the San Lucas prison (Costa Rica) and based on 17 years of being an inmate there. Describes the brutal conditions of the prison during the first part of this century, and reflects the strong desire for life and freedom of the prisoner-author.

Cuba

132. Arcocha, Juan. *A candle in the wind.* Tr. Lenna Jones. New York: Lyle Stuart, 1967, 187 p.

(original title unavailable)

Ideological novel about post-revolutionary Cuba.

133. Arenal, Humberto. *The sun beats down; a novella of the Cuban revolution.* Tr. Joseph M. Bernstein. New York: Hill and Wang, 1959. 96 p.*

(original title: *El sol a plomo,* 1958)

Revolutionaries kidnap a Mexican boxer to embarrass the Batista government.

134. Arenas, Reinaldo. *Hallucinations; being an account of the life and adventures of Friar Servando Teresa de Mier.* Tr. Gordon Brotherston. New York: Harper and Row, 1971. 287 p. (London: Jonathan Cape, 1971)

(original title: *El mundo alucinante; una novela de aventuras,* 1969)

Translated from the French edition *Le Monde Hallucinant (Paris: Editions du Seuil,* 1968).

A complex and interesting fictionalized biography of the famous Mexican friar.

135. Cabrera Infante, Guillermo. *Three trapped tigers.* Tr. Donald Gardner and Suzanne Jill Levine, in collaboration with the author. New York: Harper and Row, 1971. 487 p.

(original title: *Tres tristes tigres,* 1967)

Set in pre-revolutionary Havana, a linguistic *tour de force* about contemporary society and the nature of language as a means of communication. A successful translation of a virtually "untranslatable" novel.

136. Carpentier, Alejo. *Explosion in a cathedral.* Tr. John Sturrock. Boston: Little, Brown, and Co., 1963. 351 p.* (London: Gollancz, 1963; rpt. Harmondsworth: Penguin, 1971)

(original title: *El siglo da las luces,* 1962)

Translation from the first French edition (1962), which was published shortly before the Spanish original.

Well constructed historical novel of the French Revolution as seen in Haiti and French Guiana.

137. _____. *The kingdom of this world.* Tr. Harriet de Onís. New York: Knopf, 1957. 150 p.* (rpt. London: Gollancz, 1967; rpt. New York: Collier Books, 1970. 186 p.)

(original title: *El reino de este mundo,* 1949)

Surrealistic touches in this novel of the struggle for independence in Haiti and the rise to power of Henri Christophe.

138. _____. *The lost steps.* Tr. Harriet de Onís. New York: Knopf, 1956. 278 p. Rev. (2nd) ed., intro J. B. Priestly, 1967. xvii, 278 p. (London: Gollancz, 1956. 278 p.; rpt. Harmondsworth: Penguin, 1968. 252 p.)

(original title: *Los pasos perdidos,* 1953)

One of the major works of Latin American "Magic Realism," set mostly in the Orinoco River region.

139. Desnoes, Edmundo. *Inconsolable memories.* Tr. by author. Foreword Jack Gelber. New York: New American Library, 1967. 155 p. * (London: Deutsch, 1968; rpt. as *Memories of underdevelopment.* Harmondsworth: Penguin, 1971)

(original title: *Memorias del subdesarrollo,* 1965)

First person narrative on Cuban life before and after the Revolution of 1959. Personal anguish of author.

140. Lezama Lima, José. *Paradiso.* Tr. Gregory Rabassa. New York: Farrar, Straus and Giroux, 1974. 466 p. (Toronto: Doubleday Canada, 1974; London: Secker & Warbury, 1974)

(original title: *Paradiso,* 1966)

Translated from the Mexican edition of the novel (México: Ediciones Era, 1968)

A linguistic *tour de force* of brilliant description and poetic evocations. An outstanding example of the Neo-Baroque element of modern Latin American literature.

141. Riera, Pepita. *Prodigy*. Anon. trans. New York: Pageant Pr., 1956. 287 p.*

(original title: *El amor que no quisiste,* 1955)
Biographical novel about Beatriz del Real during the political upheaval of the 1930's in Cuba.

142. Villaverde, Cirilo. *The quadroon, or Cecilia Valdés; a romance of old Havana*. Tr. Mariano J. Lorente. Boston: L. C. Page, 1935. 399 p.*

(original title: *Cecilia Valdés, o la loma del ángel,* 1882)
Romantic novel of racial conflicts as it documents life in Cuba during slavery.

143. _____. *Cecilia Valdés, or Angel's hill; a novel of Cuban customs*. Tr. and intro. Sydney G. Gest. Pref. by author. New York: Vantage Pr., 1962. 546 p.*

(original title (*Cecilia Valdés, o la loma del ángel*, 1882)
See No. 142.

Dominican Republic

144. Galván, Manuel de Jesús. *The cross and the sword*. Ed. and tr. Robert Graves. Foreword Max Henríquez Ureña. Bloomington: Indiana Univ. Pr., 1954. xvii, 366 p. illus. (rpt. London: Gollancz, 1956)

(original title: *Enriquillo, leyenda histórica deminicana*, 1882)
This volume was published as part of the UNESCO Collection of Representative Works of Latin America. The text includes scholarly notes by the editor and translator.

A well-documented historical novel based on the life of Bartolomé de Las Casas in Santo Domingo between 1502-1533.

Ecuador

145. Aguilera Malta, Demetrio. *Manuela la Caballeresa del Sol*. Tr. and intro. Willis Knapp Jones. Foreword J. Cary Davis. Afterword W. K. Jones. Carbonale, Illinois: Southern Illinois Univ. Pr., 1967. xvi, 304 p.

(original title: *La caballeresa del sol,* 1964)
Authorized translation of this historical novel about Simón Bolívar and his mistress, Manuela Sáenz.

146. Gil Gibert, Enrique. *Our daily bread*. Tr. Dudley Poore. New York: Farrar and Rinehart, 1943. 246 p.*

(original title: *Nuestro pan,* 1941)
Strong social thesis in novel of the exploitation of peasants in the rice fields of Ecuador.

147. Icaza, Jorge. *Huasipungo*. Tr. Mervyn Savill. London: Dobson, 1962. 171 p.

(original title: *Huasipungo,* 1934)
Tr. of the original edition in Spanish. The novel first appeared in translation by an anonymous translator in *International Literature* (Moscow, Feb. 1936).
A major *indigenista* novel of the exploitation of peasants in the Ecuadorian sierra. Characterized by crude realism and a strong social thesis. See No. 148.

148. _____. *The villagers*

(Huasipungo). Tr. and intro. Bernard M. Dulsey. Pref. Jorge Icaza. Foreword J. Cary Davis. Carbondale; Southern Illinois Univ. Pr., 1964. xv, 223 p. glossary (rpt. 1973, paper)

(original title: *Huasipungo,* 1934)
An authorized translation based on the rev. ed. of *Huasipungo,* 1957. Glossary of regionalisms, pp. [218]-223.

Guatemala

149. Asturias, Miguel Angel. *The bejeweled boy.* Tr. Martin Shuttleworth. Garden City, N.Y.: Doubleday, 1971. 188 p.*

(original title: *El alhajadito,* 1961)
Poetic novel of childhood memories by the Nobel Prize winning novelist.

150. _____. *The cyclone.* Tr. Darwin Flakoll and Claribel Alegría. London: Peter Owen, 1967. 238 p.

(original title: *Viento fuerte,* 1950)
The first of Asturias' famous "Banana Trilogy," all of which emphasize social and economic exploitation by a large North American fruit company.

151. _____. *The eyes of the interred.* Tr. Gregory Rabassa. New York: Delacorte Pr., 1973. 695 p.* (London: Cape, 1974)

(original title: *Los ojos de los enterrados,* 1960)
The third volume of the aforementioned trilogy.

152. _____. *The green pope.* Tr. Gregory Rabassa. New York:

Delacorte Pr., 1971. 386 p. (London: Cape, 1971)

(original title: *El papa verde,* 1954)
Of exploited peasants. The second volume of the "Banana Trilogy."

153. _____. *Mulata.* Tr. Gregory Rabassa. New York: Delacorte Pr., 1967. 307 p. (rpt. New York: Dell, 1968. 348 p.;* British edition entitled *The mulatta and Mister Fly.* London: Peter Owen, 1967; rpt. Harmondsworth: Penguin, 1970)

(original title: *Mulata de tal,* 1963)
Complex novel which probes the mythical and magical nature of Guatemalan reality.

154. _____. *El Señor Presidente.* Tr. Frances Partridge. New York: Atheneum, 1964. 287 p. (Published previously as *The President.* London: Victor Gollancz, 1963; rpt. Harmondsworth: Penguin, 1972)

(original title: *El Señor Presidente,* 1946)
Asturias' first and most famous novel, winner of the Ibero-American Novel Award of the William Faulkner Foundation (1962). Successful and innovative use of the language in a novel of terror and corruption.

155. _____. *Strong wind.* Tr. Gregory Rabassa. New York: Delacorte Pr., 1968. 242 p.

(original title: *Viento fuerte,* 1950)
American edition by prize-winning translator Rabassa. See No. 91.

156. Ayala, Robert H. *Quarter to six.* Tr. Emil G. Beavers. New York: Exposition Pr., 1955. 186 p.*

(original title unavailable)

A rather melodramatic love story set in the United States and Guatemala.

Honduras

157. Díaz Lozano, Argentina. *Henriqueta and I.* Tr. Harriet de Onís. New York: Farrar and Rinehart, 1944. 217 p. illus.*

(original title: *Peregrinaje*, 1944)
An autobiographical novel.

158. _____. *Mayapan.* Tr. Lydia Wright. Indian Hills, Colorado: Falcon's Wing Pr., 1955. 247 p.*

(original title: *Mayapán*, 1950)
A historical novel of her native Honduras.

Mexico

159. Altamirano, Ignacio M. *Christmas in the mountains.* Ed., tr. and intro. Harvey L. Johnson. Gainesville: Univ. of Florida Pr., 1961. 68 p. Bibliog.*

(original title: *Navidad en las montañas*, 1871)
An idyllic, romantic novelette set in rural village.

160. _____. *El Zarco, the bandit.* Tr. Mary Allt. New York: Duchnes, 1957. 160 p.* (London: Folio Society, 1957)

(original title: *El Zarco,* 1901)
Emphasizes the equality of the mestizo and Indian compared to the Anglo-Saxon.

161. Azuela, Mariano. *Marcela; a Mexican love story.* Tr. Anita Brenner. Foreword Waldo Frank. New York: Farrar and Rinehart, 1932. xi, 244 p.*

(original title: *Mala yerba*, 1909)
One of the better of Azuela's early novels characterized by literary realism dealing with the poor.

162. _____. *Two novels of Mexico: 'The flies' and 'The bosses'.* Tr. and intro. Lesley Byrd Simpson. Berkeley: Univ. of California Pr., 1957. xiii, 194 p. (London: Cambridge Univ. Pr., 1956)

(original titles: *Las moscas*, 1918; *Los caciques*, 1917)
Two short novels of the Mexican Revolution.

163. _____. *Two novels of .he Mexican Revolution: 'The trials of a respectable family' and 'The underdogs'.* Tr. Frances Kellam Hendricks and Beatrice Berler. Prol. Salvador Azuela. San Antonio, Texas: Principia Pr. of Trinity Univ. (Trinity Univ. Pr.), 1963. xxvii, 267 p.*

(original titles: *Las tribulaciones de una familia decente*, 1919; *Los de abajo*, 1916)
"The trials" is one of Azuela's better novelistic chronicles of life during the time of the Mexican Revolution. Regarding the second novel, see No. 164.

164. _____. *The underdogs.* Tr. Enrique Mungía, Jr. Pref. Carleton Beals. New York: Brentano's, 1929. xviii, 225 p. (rpt., with foreword by Harriet de Onís in replacement of

Beals' preface, New York: New American Library, 1963. xi, 151 p. bibliog. paper

(original title: *Los de abajo,* 1916)
"Selected Bibliography," p. 151 (list of his novels).
The classic novel of the Mexican Revolution, translated into almost every major living language.

165. Benítez, Fernando. *The poisoned water (El agua envenenada).* Tr. Mary E. Ellsworth. Foreword J. Carey Davis. Carbondale, Illinois: Southern Illinois Univ. Pr., 1973. vii, 152 p.

(original title: *El agua envenenada,* 1961)
Of a village's bloody rebellion against its autocratic leader, based on an actual event.

166. Carballido, Emilio. *The Norther (El norte).* Tr. and intro. Margaret Sayers Peden. Austin: Univ. of Texas Pr., 1968. 101 p. illus.

(original title: *El norte,* 1958)
An excellent study of human relationships involving 3 characters.

167. Castellanos, Rosario. *The nine guardians.* Tr. Irene Nicholson. New York: Vanguard, 1960. 272 p. (London: Faber and Faber, 1959)

(original title: *Balún-Canán*, 1957)
An *indigenista* novel of rural Mexico.

168. Fernández de Lizardi, José Joaquín. *The itching parrot (El periquillo sarniento).* Tr., ed. and intro. Katherine Anne Porter. Garden City, N.Y.: Doubleday, Doran, 1942. xliii, 290 p. *

(original title: *El periquillo sarniento*, 1816)
Includes a long introduction, "Notes on the life and death of a hero," pp. xiii-xliii. An abridged edition, of only 33 selected chapters, with much editing of political pamphlets and moral disquisitions.
Considered to be the first Spanish American novel, written as a picaresque account of a young man to adulthood.

169. Fuentes, Carlos. *Aura.* Tr. Lysander Kemp. New York: Farrar, Straus and Giroux, 1965. 74 p.*

(original title: *Aura,* 1962)
A short novel of phantasmagorical dimensions.

170. _____. *A change of skin.* Tr. Sam Hileman. New York: Farrar, Straus, and Giroux, 1968. (London: Cape, 1968; Rexdale, Ontario: Ambassador Books, 1968; rpt. New York: Putnam, 1970)

(original title: *Cambio de piel,* 1967)
Fuentes' most ambitious novel, combining a multiplicity of narrative techniques in a powerful vision of Mexico's history and society.

171. _____. *The death of Artemio Cruz.* Tr. Sam Hileman. New York: Farrar, Straus and Giroux, 1964. 306 p. (London: Collins, 1964. 254 p.; rpt. New York: Noonday Pr., 1966. paper; rpt. London: Panther, 1969. paper)

(original title: *La muerte de Artemio Cruz,* 1962)
Social criticism developed in the evocations of Artemio's past, seen from varying points of view.

172. Fuentes, Carlos. *The good conscience.* Tr. [Sam Hileman]. New York: Ivan Obolensky, 1961. 148 p. (rpt. New York: Noonday Pr., 1961, paper)

(original title: *Las buenas conciencias*, 1959)
Uncomplicated novel set in the epoch of Porfirio Díaz of the life of a family in Guanajuato, and the religious and moral crisis of an adolescent boy.

173. _____. *Where the air is clear.* Tr. Sam Hileman. New York: Ivan Obolensky, 1960. 376 p. (Toronto: George J. McLeod, 1960; rpt. New York: Noonday Pr., 1971. paper)

(original title: *La región más transparente*, 1958)
Vision of life in Mexico City during the 1950's in which characters seek a sense of personal and national identity.

174. Galindo, Sergio. *The precipice (El bordo).* Tr. John and Carolyn Brushwood. Intro. John Brushwood. Austin: Univ. of Texas Pr., 1969. xiii, 185 p. illus.

(original title: *El bordo,* 1960)
Presents one family and the eventual tragedy they endure. Set in Mexico but without emphasis to Mexican landscape, problems, history.

175. Garro, Elena. *Recollections of things to come (Los recuerdos del porvenir).* Tr. and intro. Ruth L. C. Simms. Austin: Univ. of Texas Pr., 1969. x, 289 p. illus.

(original title: *Los recuerdos del porvenir,* 1963)
Successful combination of realism and magical events in a novel of post-revolutionary Mexico in a rural town.

176. Guzmán, Martín Luis. *The eagle and the serpent.* Tr. Harriet de Onís. New York: Knopf, 1930. ix, 359 p.; rev. ed. (with intro. Federico de Onís and foreword by author). Garden City, N.Y.: Doubleday. 1965. xiv, 386 p. (rpt. Gloucester, Mass.: Peter Smith, 1969)

(original title: *El águila y la serpiente*, 1928)
The 1930 edition is a slightly abridged translation.
Chronicle of life with Pancho Villa during the Mexican Revolution.

177. _____. *Memoirs of Pancho Villa.* Tr. Virginia H. Taylor. Pref. by author. Austin: Univ. of Texas Pr., 1965. xii, 512 p.

(original title: *Memorias de Pancho Villa,* 1938-1940)
A condensed translation, eliminating redundancies. Includes an extensive index of names and places, pp. 483-512.
Revolutionary hero Pancho Villa narrates in first person events of the Mexican Revolution between 1910 and 1914.

178. López y Fuentes, Gregorio. *El indio.* Tr. Anita Brenner. Pref. Lynn Carrick. Indianapolis, Ind.: Bobbs-Merrill, 1937. 256 p. illus. (As *They that reap.* London: Harrap, 1937; rpt. of American ed. New York: Ungar, 1961)

(original title: *El indio,* 1935)
Illustrations by famous Mexican artist Diego Rivera.
Of the continued suffering and exploitation of the peasant class even after the Mexican Revolution.

179. Magdaleno, Mauricio. *Sunburst.* Tr. Anita Brenner. New York: Viking Pr., 1944. 290 p.*

(original title: *El resplandor,* 1937)
A novel of post-revolutionary Mexico which stresses the betrayal of revolutionary ideals.

180. Márquez Campos, Alfredo. *I wouldn't dare.* Tr. Juan Berlier. New York: Vantage, 1965. 229 p.*

(original title: *Yo no haría eso,* 1956)
A popular novel of scant literary merit.

181. Menéndez, Miguel Angel. *Nayar.* Tr. Angel Flores. New York: Farrar and Rinehart, 1942. 277 p.*

(original title: *Nayar,* 1940)
Indigenista novel.

182. Mondragón Aguirre, Magdalena. *Some day the dream.* Tr. Samuel Putnam. New York: Dial Pr., 1947. 240 p. *

(original title: *Yo como pobre,* 1944)
A realist novel of slum life in Mexico City by well-known journalist Mondragón. Expresses the author's protest of social conditions.

183. Revueltas, José. *The stone knife.* Tr. H. R. Hays. New York: Reynal and Hitchcock, 1947. viii, 183 p.*

(original title: *El luto humano,* 1943)
A flood threatens the lives of rural peasants, whose memories of the Revolution and new political struggles add to their suffering.

184. Romero, José Rubén. *The futile life of Pito Pérez.* Tr. William O. Cord. Englewood Cliffs, N.J.: Prentice-Hall, 1966. vi, 151 p. illus.

(original title: *La vida inútil de Pito Pérez,* 1938)
A modern *pícaro,* Pito Pérez seeks goodness in a hopelessly corrupt and ugly world.

185. Rulfo, Juan. *Pedro Páramo.* Tr. Lysander Kemp. New York: Grove Pr., 1959. 123 p. (London: Calder, 1959; rpt. New York: Grove (Evergreen), 1969. paper)

(original title: *Pedro Páramo,* 1955)
The celebrated masterpiece of a search for Paradise which ends instead in the infernal atmosphere of Comala.

186. Sáinz, Gustavo. *Gazapo.* Tr. Hardie St. Martin. New York: Farrar, Straus and Giroux, 1968. 179 p.*

(original title: *Gazapo,* 1965)
A technically excellent novel which analyzes the nature of love in contemporary society. By a highly regarded member of the new generation of Mexican novelists.

187. Spota, Luis. *Almost paradise.* Tr. Roy and Renate Morrison. Garden City, N.Y.: Doubleday, 1963. 391 p. (rpt. New York: Paperback Library, 1964)*

(original title: *Casi el paraíso,* 1956)
A phony Italian prince tries to impress the upper crust of Mexican society. A condemnation of cafe society in Mexico City.

188. Spota, Luis. *The enemy blood.* Tr. Robert Malloy. Garden City, N.Y.: Doubleday, 1961. 308 p.* (rpt. London: Muller, 1961. 287 p.; rpt. Harmondsworth, England: Penguin, 1967. 252 p. paper)

(original title: *La sangre enemiga,* 1959)
Violent, sordid novel of an impotent man, the woman he loves, and slum society.

189. _____. *The time of wrath.* Tr. Robert Malloy. Garden City, N.Y.: Doubleday, 1962. 472 p.*

(original title: *El tiempo de la ira,* 1960)
Of a revolutionary hero who is assassinated. A fairly objective study of the nature of a dictatorship, and one of Spota's better novels.

190. _____. *The wounds of hunger.* Tr. and ed. Barnaby Conrad. Boston: Houghton-Mifflin, 1957. x, 257 p. * (rpt. London: Muller, 1958. 256 p.; New York: New American Library, 1959; Harmondsworth, England: Penguin, 1961. 207 p.)

(original title: *Más cornadas da el hambre*, 1951)
Regarded as one of the best "bullfight novels" ever written.

191. Suárez Carreño, José. *The final hours.* Tr. Anthony Kerrigan. New York: Knopf, 1954. 273 p. (rpt. New York: New American Library, 1955. 194 p.)*

(original title: *Las últimas horas*, 1950)
Usually studied as a Spanish novelist, Suárez Carreño was born in Guadalupe, Mexico.
Shows influence of Faulkner and Dos Passos, and does not sacrifice style for social content.

192. Yáñez, Agustín. *The edge of the storm (Al filo del agua).* Tr. Ethel Brinton, Austin: Univ. of Texas Pr., 1963. 332 p. illus.

(original title: *Al filo del agua,* 1947)
Using the technique of stream of consciousness with success, the author studies the life of a small town in Jalisco shortly before the Revolution.

193. _____. *The lean lands (Las tierras flacas).* Tr. Ethel Brinton. Austin: Univ. of Texas Pr., 1968. ix, 328 p.*

(original title: *Las tierras flacas,* 1962)
Studies the psychological changes of the peasant as he is affected by the age of technology and industry.

Paraguay

194. Roa Bastos, Augusto [Antonio]. *Son of man.* Tr. Rachel Caffyn. London: Gollancz, 1965. 256 p.*

(original title: *Hijo de hombre,* 1961)
An outstanding novel of popular resistance to dictatorship in Paraguay covering about a century from the nineteenth century to the Chaco war. The author combines symbols and myth in a moving, lyrical work.

Peru

195. Alegría, Ciro. *Broad and alien is the world.* Tr. Harriet de Onís. New York-Toronto: Farrar and Rinehart, 1941. 434 p. (rpt. Philadelphia: Dufour, 1962; London: Merlin Pr.,

1962; New York: Holt, Rinehart and Winston, 1963)*

(original title: *El mundo es ancho y ajeno,* 1941)
Classic *indigenista* novel of the Peruvian sierra.

196. Alegría, Ciro. *The golden serpent.* Tr. Harriet de Onís. New York-Toronto: Farrar and Rinehart, 1943. 242 p. (rpt. New York: New American Library, 1963. 192 p.)*

(original title: *La serpiente de oro,* 1935)
Important novel set in the Marañón River region.

197. Matto de Turner, Clorinda. *Birds without a nest; a story of Indian life and priestly oppression in Peru.* Tr. J. G. Hudson, London: C. J. Thynne, 1904. ix, 236 p.

(original title: *Aves sin nido,* 1889)
Combines Romantic plot and Realist detail in the first *indigenista* novel of contemporary life.

198. Vargas Llosa, Mario. *The Green House.* Tr. Gregory Rabassa. New York: Harper and Row, 1968. 405 p. (London: Cape, 1969; rpt. New York: Avon, 1973. 383 p. paper)

(original title: *La Casa Verde,* 1965)
Brilliant novel set in the Peruvian jungle and the northern coastal city of Piura. One of the principal works of the wave of outstanding recent Latin American novels.

199. _____. *The time of the hero.* Tr. Lysander Kemp. New York: Grove Pr., 1966. 409 p.* (rpt. London: Cape, 1967; London: Rapp and

Carroll, 1967; Harmondsworth: Penguin, 1971. 364 p. paper)

(original title: *La ciudad y los perros,* 1962)
A military school becomes a microcosm of Peruvian society. Copies of the author's first novel were burned by Peruvian military officials.

Puerto Rico

200. Laguerre, Enrique A. *The labyrinth.* Tr. William Rose. New York: Las Americas, 1960. 275 p.*

(original title: *El laberinto,* 1959)
About the Puerto Rican community in New York and set in New York and Santo Domingo during the Trujillo regime.

201. Soto, Pedro Juan *Hot land, cold season.* Tr. Helen R. Lane. New York: Dell, 1973. 224 p. paper

(original title: *Ardiente suelo, fría estación*, 1961)
An eighteen year old student leaves Puerto Rico to go to New York and suffers rejection there and upon his return to the island.

Uruguay

202. Amorim, Enrique Manuel. *The horse and his shadow.* Tr. James Graham Luján and Richard L. O'Connell. New York: Scribner's, 1943. x, 252 p.*

original title: *El caballo y su sombra*, 1941)
Conflict between immigrant and creole landowners.

203. Benedetti, Mario. *The truce.* Tr.

Benjamin Graham. New York: Harper and Row, 1969. 184 p.*

(original title: *La tregua,* 1960)
Excellent presentation of the frustrated quest for values and happiness in contemporary society.

204. Fonseca, Rodolfo Lucio. *Tower of ivory.* Tr. Walter Starkie. New York: J. Messner, 1954. 279 p.* (London: Cape, 1954. 251 p.)

(original title: *Turris ebúrnea,* 1947)
A strong statement against the cruel affects of war.

205. Onetti, Juan Carlos. *The shipyard.* Tr. Rachel Caffyn. New York: Scribner's, 1968. 190 p.*

(original title: *El astillero,* 1961)
Prize-winning novel of disillusionment and corruption, and meaningless goals of modern society.

206. Reyles, Carlos. *Castanets.* Tr. Jacquest Le Clercq. London-New York: Longmans, Green, 1929. 297 p. (rpt. New York: Jacobsen, 1929)*

(original title: *El embrujo de Sevilla,* 1922)
Considered to be a major work of Modernist prose. Set in Sevilla, this novel was very well received by Spanish critics as a perceptive vision of Spanish life.

207. Schroeder, Agustina. *Mother of fair love.* Tr. Veronica Kirtland. Milwaukee: Bruce, 1957. 195 p.*

(original title unavailable)
A fictionalized biography of Mary and the Holy Family.

Venezuela

208. Blanco Fombona, Rufino. *The man of gold.* Tr. Isaac Goldberg. New York: Brentano's, 1920. xii, 319 p.*

(original title: *El hombre de oro,* 1915)
Characterized by fiery criticism of Venezuelan politics and society. Representative of his severely critical essays, but of little esthetic value.

209. Díaz Sánchez, Ramón. *Cumboto.* Tr. John Upton. Austin: Univ. of Texas Pr., 1969. xii, 273 p. illus. glossary.
(original title: *Cumboto; cuento de siete leguas,* 1950)
Glossary of Venezuelan terms, pp. (272)-273.
Chosen by the Ibero-American Novel Project of the William Faulkner Foundation as the most notable novel published in Ibero-America between 1945 and 1962.
Stylized novel of Venezuelan customs and places set in the cacao producing region of the country.

210. Gallegos, Rómulo. *Doña Barbara.* Tr. Robert Malloy. New York: Cape and H. Smith, 1931. vi, 440 p. (rpt. New York: Peter Smith, 1948).

(original title: *Doña Bárbara*, 1929)
The classic Venezuelan novel of the *llanos* (plains) which depicts the Latin American theme of the struggle between civilization and barbarism.

211. Parra, Teresa de la [Ana Teresa Parra Sanojo]. *Mama Blanca's souvenirs.* Tr. Harriet de Onís. Washington, D.C.: Pan American Union, 1959. xix, 129 p.*

(original title: *Las memorias de Mamá Blanca*, 1929)

Of the UNESCO Collection of Representative Works of Latin American Literature.

Nostalgic memoirs of life on a sugar cane plantation near Caracas which give insight into the spirit and character of a fading aristocracy.

212. Prato, Luis F. *Wind Storm: A novel of the Venezuelan Andes.* Tr. Hugh Jencks. New York: Las Americas, 1961. 221 p.*

(original title: *Ventisca,* 1953)

Good description of the physical characteristics of the Andean region, but less successful in character development.

213. Uslar Pietri, Arturo. *The red lances.* Tr. Harriet de Onís. New York: Knopf, 1963. 233 p.*

(original title: *Las lanzas coloradas,* 1931)

Excellent novel of the war of independence in Venezuela. Mention is made of Bolívar, but he does not appear as a character.

2. Short Stories

Argentina

214. Anderson Imbert, Enrique. *The other side of the mirror (El grimorio).* Tr. and intro. Isabel Reade. Foreword J. Cary Davis. Carbondale: Southern Illinois Univ. Pr., 1966. xiii, 226 p.* (rpt. London: Mac-Donald, 1968)

Authorized translation of *El grimorio* (1961), a collection of stories by the noted contemporary critic and author.

215. Benedetto, Antonio di. *Declinación y ángel; Decline and angel.* Prol. Luis Emilio Soto. Mendoza, Argentina: Biblioteca Pública San Martín, 1958. 111 p.

A bilingual edition of short stories.

216. _____. *Two stories.* Tr. (Marta M. de Sabisch) and (Susana Tampieri de Estrella). Intro. Abelardo Arias, Alfonso Sola González *et al.* Mendoza, Argentina: Voces, 1965. 60 p. illus.

A bilingual edition (English section, pp. 7-34).

The stories are: "The abandon and the passivity" ("El abandono y la pasividad") and "Horse in the salt flat" ("Caballo en el salitral"). In the intro. Benedetto is called the first "Objectivist" writer in the Spanish language, and a precursor of French Objectivism.

217. Bioy Casares, Adolfo. *The invention of Morel; and other stories from 'La trama celeste'.* Tr. Ruth L. C. Simms. Prol. Jorge Luis Borges. Austin: Univ. of Texas Pr., 1964. 237 p. illus.*

Tr. of *La invención de Morel* (1940) and *La trama celeste* (1948).

Borges introduces his friend and collaborator and discusses "The invention of Morel" in terms of the adventure story in Latin American and world literature of the twentieth century. Six selections from *La trama celeste.*

218. Borges, Jorge Luis. *The Aleph and other stories, 1933-1969; together with commentaries and an autobiographical essay.* Ed. and tr. Norman Thomas di Giovanni in collab. with the author. New York:

E. P. Dutton, 1970. 286 p. bibliog. (rpt. London: Cape, 1971. 188 p.; rpt. New York: Bantam, 1971. 210 p. paper; rpt. London: Pan Books, 1973. 188 p. paper)

An important collection of 20 stories, including those of *El Aleph* (1957). Well annotated. "An autobiographical essay" and "Commentaries" are English originals especially prepared for the English edition.

219. Borges, Jorge Luis. *The congress.* Tr. Norman Thomas di Giovanni in collab. with the author. London: Enitharmon Pr., 1973.

(original title: *El congreso*, 1971)
A world congress is called. As in Borges' even shorter works of fiction or fictional essays, the complexity of human existence is treated in typically Borgesian style.

220. _____. *Doctor Brodie's report.* Tr. Norman Thomas di Giovanni in collab. with the author. New York: E. P. Dutton, 1972. 128 p. (rpt. New York: Bantam, 1973. xiii, 154 p., paper; rpt. London: Allen Lane, 1974. 128 p.)

Includes the stories of *El informe de Brodie* (1970) and a revised trans. of "The intruder" (La intrusa) from *El Aleph* (1957). Total of 11 stories. An afterword, prepared for the English edition, is followed by a brief bibliographical note about the sources of this edition. All of the Di Giovanni-Borges translations are carefully prepared with extensive bibliographical notes and references.

221. _____. *Dreamtigers.* Tr. Mildred Boyer and Harold Morland. Intro. Miguel Enguídanos. Austin: Univ. of Texas Pr., 1964. 95 p. illus. (rpt. with pref. Victor Lange. New York: E. P. Dutton, 1970. xxxi, 95 p. (no illus.), paper; rpt. Toronto: Clark and Irwin, 1970; rpt. London: Souvenir Pr., 1973)

Trans. of *El Hacedor* (1960), a collection of 24 prose selections (tr. Boyer) and 31 poems (tr. Morland). Does not include Spanish originals of the poems. An appendix, "Some facts in the life of Jorge Luis Borges," is included.

222. _____. *Ficciones.* Ed. and intro. Anthony Kerrigan. London: Weidenfeld and Nicolson, 1962. 174 p. (rpt. New York: Grove Pr., 1963; rpt. London: Calder, 1965. 159 p.)

Trans. of *Ficciones* (1956). Various translators. An outstanding collection of Borges' prose, and one of the first works in English translation which contributed to the high esteem with which he is regarded in the English-speaking world. Includes stories and essays.

_____. *In praise of darkness.* See No. 267.

223. _____. *Labyrinths; selected stories and other writings.* Ed. Donald A. Yates and James E. Irby. Intro. James E. Irby, Pref. André Maurois. New York: New Directions. 1962. 248 p.; Augmented ed., 1964. xxiii, 260 p. bibliog. (rpt. of 1964 ed. Harmondsworth, England: Penguin, 1970. 297 p.)
Various translators. Includes a chronology of Borges' life and a bibliography of original works and criticism.
The collection includes 23 "fictions," 10 essays, 8 parables and 1

elegy, selected from *Ficciones* (1956), *El Aleph* (1957), *Discusión* (1957), *Otras inquisiciones* (1960, and *El Hacedor* (1960). The works are well chosen and provide an excellent volume of representative selections.

224. Borges, Jorge Luis. *A personal anthology*. Ed. and foreword Anthony Kerrigan. Prol. Jorge Luis Borges. New York: Grove Pr., 1967. xiii, 210 p. (rpt. London: Cape, 1968; rpt. London: Pan Books, 1972. xii, 179 p.)

Various translators collaborate in the trans. of *Antología personal* (1961). The volume includes 20 poems and 28 prose selections chosen by the author from several works. It ends with an epilogue by the editor: an exchange of letters between Anthony Kerrigan and Alastair Reid (one of the translators).

225. _____. *A universal history of infamy*. Tr. Norman Thomas di Giovanni. New York: E. P. Dutton, 1972. 146 p. bibliog. (rpt. Toronto: Clarke, Irwin, 1972; rpt. London: Allen Lane, 1973)

A trans. of the 2nd ed. of *Historia universal de la infamia* (1954), a rev. ed. of the original of the same title (1935).

Includes the pref. to both the original edition and the 2nd ed. Contains 7 selections of "A universal history of infamy," "Etcetera" (7 selections), and Borges' first short story, "Street corner man" ("El hombre de la esquina rosada").

As an added bibliographical bonus, the volume includes a list of sources of the original edition (stories of infamy from which he bases his own) and a note ("Original titles and first newspaper or magazine appearances of the pieces").

226. _____ and Adolfo Bioy Casares, ed. *Extraordinary tales*. Ed., tr. and foreword of English ed. Anthony Kerrigan. New York: Herder and Herder, 1971. 144 p.*

Trans. of *Cuentos breves y extraordinarios* (1967), an anthology of fantastic tales from many countries and periods. Although it does not include fiction by Borges, it does show his interest in and knowledge of these works. The collections contain works by Virgilio Piñera (Cuba), Adolfo Bioy Casares (Argentina), Silvina Ocampo (Argentina), Manuel Peyrou (Argentina), Alfonso Reyes (Mexico), and many others.

227. _____ and Margarita Guerrero. *The book of imaginary beings*. Rev. and enlarged ed. Tr. Norman Thomas di Giovanni in collab. with the author. New York: E. P. Dutton, 1969. 256 p. (rpt. London: Cape, 1970; rpt. New York: Avon, 1970)

The English edition is rewritten and expanded by Borges and Di Giovanni. Originally published as *Manual de zoología fantástica* (1957) with 82 selections, the book was expanded with the addition of 34 more pieces under the title of *El libro de los seres imaginarios* (1967). The English ed. includes many altered articles and 4 which appear for the first time, written originally in English.

The volume contains 3 prefaces and an index.

Borges' bestiary not only reveals his penchant for the fantastic and his knowledge of world literature, but also highlights the wit and intellectual curiosity with which he views man and his universe.

228. Cortázar, Julio. *All fires the fire, and other stories.* Tr. Suzanne Jill Levine. New York: Pantheon Pr., 1973. 152 p.

A trans. of *Todos los fuegos el fuego* (1966), a collection of 8 stories by one of the leading exponents of contemporary Latin American fiction.

229. _____. *End of the game and other stories.* Tr. Paul Blackburn. New York: Pantheon Pr., 1967. 277 p.* (rpt. London: Collins, 1968; rpt. London: Harvill Pr., 1968; rpt. as *Blow up, and other stories.* New York: Collier Books, 1968. 248 p. paper)

A representative selection of short stories from the author's early collections: *Bestiario* (1951), *Las armas secretas* (1959), and *Final del juego* (1956). Includes a total of 15 stories.

230. _____. *Cronopois and famas.* Tr. Paul Blackburn. New York: Pantheon Pr., 1969. 161 p.

(original title: *Historia de cronopios y de famas,* 1962)
Seemingly a series of nonsensical stories, they reveal Cortázar's concern for living an authentic and committed life.

231. Echeverría, Esteban. *El matadero (The slaughterhouse).* Ed. and tr. Angel Flores. New York: Las Americas, (1959). 37 p. bibliog.*

(original title: *El matadero,* 1871)
A bilingual edition, parallel texts. Includes a brief biographical sketch with a bibliography of selected works of criticism on Echeverría (pp. 36-37).

The story was written near 1840, but because it is a symbolic attack on the regime of dictator Rosas, it was not published until after the author's death.

232. Gerchunoff, Alberto. *The Jewish gauchos of the pampas.* Tr. Prudencio de Pereda. New York-London: Abelar-Schuman, 1955. 169 p. Rev. ed. 1959. xvii, 169 p. illus.*

Trans. of *Los gauchos judíos* (1910), stories of Jewish immigrants in Argentina.

233. Mallea, Eduardo. *All green shall perish, and other novellas and stories.* Ed. and intro. John B. Hughes. Tr. by editor *et al.* New York: Knopf, 1966. xxiii, 431 p.

An impressive selection of 3 short novels and 4 short stories. Various translators.
Novels include: *Fiesta in November* (*Fiesta en noviembre,* 1938), *All green shall perish* (*Todo verdor perecerá,* 1941), and *Chaves* (*Chaves,* 1953). Each title was published separately in England. See individual titles.
This is a valuable contribution to the bibliography of Argentine letters in English translation, for it makes a significant number of representative works of fiction by Mallea accessible to the English-speaking public.

234. _____. *Chaves, and other stories.* Tr. María Mercedes Aspiazu *et al.* London: Calder and Boyars, 1970. 190 p.

Originally published in Mallea's *All green shall perish, and other novellas and stories.* See No. 233.

235. Vigil, Constancio C. *The adventures of Hormiguita.* Tr. Gilda Massa. Forest Hills, N.Y.: Las Americas, 1943. 49 p. illus.*

A bilingual edition of *La hormiguita viajera* (1940).

Chile

236. Lillo, Baldomero. *The Devil's pit, and other stories.* Ed. and tr. Esther S. Dillon and Angel Flores. Washington, D.C.: Pan American Union, 1959. xxxii, 152 p.*

Part of the UNESCO Collection of Representative Works of Latin American Literature.
The collection includes stories from *Sub terra* (1904), *Cuadros mineros, Sub sole* (1907), and *Relatos populares.* Examples of the regionalistic prose of Creolism in Chilean letters.

237. Mistral, Gabriela [Lucila Godoy Alcayaga]. *Crickets and frogs; a fable. Grillos y ranas; una fábula.* Tr. and adapted Doris Dana. New York: Atheneum, 1972. 1 vol. unpaged. [31 p.]
A bilingual children's story of a vocal duel between crickets and frogs.

238. Subercaseaux, Benjamín. *From West to East; five stories.* Ed. and tr. John Garret Underhill. New York: Putnam, 1940. vii, 215 p.*

Tr. of two works: *Y al oeste limita con el mar* (1937) and *Rahab* (1938). Four stories from the former ("West") and the longer story "Rahab" ("East").
Subercaseaux developed a great interest in the cultures and philosophies of the East as a result of many travels, but he continued to write of his native Chile.

Colombia

239. García Márquez, Gabriel. *Leaf storm, and other stories.* Tr. Gregory Rabassa. New York: Harper and Row, 1972. 146 p. (rpt. London: Cape, 1972; rpt. New York: Avon, 1974. paper)

Trans. of the title story (*La hojarasca,* 1955) and 6 stories from various sources. Provides another look at the imaginary world of Macondo.

240. _____. *No one writes to the Colonel, and other stories.* Tr. J. S. Bernstein. New York: Harper and Row, 1968. v, 170 p. (rpt. London: Cape, 1971; rpt. Harmondsworth, England: Penguin, 1974. 157 p. paper; rpt. New York: Avon, 1974. paper)

A trans. of the novelette *El coronel no tiene quien le escriba* (1962) and 8 stories from *Los funerales de la Mamá Grande* (1962).
An important collection of stories which develop the view of mythical Macondo, and thus serve to introduce and complement García Márquez' outstanding novel *Cien años de soledad (One hundred years of solitude).* By a recognized master.

Costa Rica

241. Fernández Guardia, Ricardo. *Costa Rican tales.* Tr. Gray Casement. Rev. tr. and intro. Isaac Goldberg. Girard, Kansas: Haldeman-Julius, 1925. 62 p.*

Contains 3 stories originally tr. by

Mr. Casement in *Cuentos ticos; short stories of Costa Rica.* See No. 237.

Goldberg's rev. translations include "A miraculous saint," "Politics," and "Chivalry."

242. _____. *Cuentos ticos; short stories of Costa Rica.* Tr. and intro. Gray Casement. Cleveland: Burrows, 1904. 293 p. 2nd ed., 1905. 3rd ed., 1925. 307 p. illus. maps. (rpt. of 3rd ed. Freeport, N.Y.: Books for Libraries Pr., 1970)*

Collection of 10 stories from *Cuentos ticos* (1901). Only "Un alma" is omitted in the English ed. The intro. deals with Costa Rica, not with the works of the author.

Cuba

243. Carpentier, Alejo. *War of time.* Tr. Frances Partridge. New York: Knopf, 1970. 179 p. (rpt. London: Victor Gollancz, 1970; rpt. Toronto: Random House of Canada, 1970)

Includes 3 stories originally published in *Guerra del tiempo* (1963) and 2 which appear for the first time in the expanded French edition, *Guerre du Temps* (1967).
Stories include: "Like the night," "Journey back to the source," "The highroad of St. James" (all from *Guerra del tiempo*), and "Right of Sanctuary" and "The chosen" *(Guerre du Temps).*
Missing is the novellette *El acoso* (Manhunt) which appears in *Guerra del tiempo.*
The "war of time" referred to in the title deals with the innovative manner in which the author deals with the problem of time in each narrative.

244. Montaner, Carlos Alberto. *The witches' poker game, and other stories. The edge of the abyss.* Tr. Robert L. Robinson. Hato Rey, Puerto Rico: Inter-American Univ. Pr., 1973. 171 p. paper.

Trans. of two collections: *Poker de brujas* (1967) and *Instantáneas al borde del abismo* (1970). Stories of madness, the macabre, black humor.

Guatemala

245. Asturias, Miguel Angel. *The talking machine.* Tr. and adapted Beverly Koch. Garden City, N.Y.: Doubleday, 1971. 48 p. illus.

Published as a story for children. A translation of "La máquina de hablar" in *El alhajadito* (1961). A young frog purchases a "Talking machine."

246. Monterroso, Augusto. *The black sheep and other fables.* Tr. Walter I. Bradbury. Garden City, N.Y.: Doubleday, 1971. 112 p. illus.*

(original title: *La oveja negra y demás fábulas,* 1969)
Translations made with cooperation of the author. Contains a useful onomastic and geographical index.
A collection of 40 fables, a genre cultivated by few Latin American writers.

247. Samayoa Chinchilla, Carlos. *The emerald lizard: Tales and legends of Guatemala.* Tr. Joan Coyne MacLean. Indian Hills, Colorado: The Falcon's Wing Pr., 1957. 274 p. illus.*

Trans. of stories and legends from *Madre Milpa* (1950). Includes "The birth of Corn" (tr. Harriet de Onís) which first appeared in translation in *The golden land* (see No. 7). Illustrated by the author.

Samayoa Chinchilla retells popular legends, colonial tales, and contemporary stories, or bases his narrations on them. A combination of folklore and original prose.

Mexico

248. Arreola, Juan José. *Confabulario and other inventions*. Tr. and intro. George D. Schade. Austin: Univ. of Texas Pr., 1964. xviii, 245 p. illus. (rpt. 1974, paper)

Translations follow the edition of *Confabulario total* (1962) of prose selections published between 1949 and 1962. Omitted are "La hora de todos" (a one-act play) and "Balada." The order of the works is also altered by the translator. The almost 100 prose selections are characterized by a mixture of genres and by the author's wit and humor.

249. Gómez Rul, Ana María. *Lol-Ha; a Maya tale*. México: Editorial Cultura, 1935. 45 p.

Purportedly a Maya tale, but apparently a creation of the author. An idealized, Romantic story of an Indian princess who eventually marries a prince.

A glossary, "Translations of the Maya words to English" (p. 45) is of some use.

250. Martínez Cáceres, Arturo. *In memoriam: Mexican short stories*. Tr. D. O. Chambers. New York: Vantage Pr., 1967. 117 p.*

A trans. of the 11 short stories of *In memoriam* (2nd ed. 1967), originally published in 1960.

251. Médiz Bolio, Antonio. *The land of the pheasant and the deer*. Tr. Enid E. Perkins. México: Cultura, 1935. 155 p. illus.

Trans. of *La tierra del faisán y del venado* (1922), poetic prose based on Maya legends and myths.

252. Rubín, Ramón. *Don Sóstenes treasure; a Mexican short story*. Tr. Rosemary Holt. Guadalajara, México: Contemporary Editions, 1959? 32 p. illus.

A very limited edition of one story by *indigentista* novelist Rubín.

253. _____. *His heroic dog; a Mexican short story*. Tr. Rosemary Holt. Guadalajara, México: contemporary Editions, 1959? 29 p. illus.

254. Rulfo, Juan. *The burning plain and other stories*. Tr. and intro. George D. Schade. Austin: Univ. of Texas Pr., 1967. xv, 175 p. illus. (rpt. 1971, paper)

Trans. of *El llano en llamas* (1953). Fifteen stories which complement the novel *Pedro Páramo* in describing the harsh, desperate condition of the rural poor in Mexico. By one of Latin America's leading fiction writers.

Nicaragua

255. Calderón Ramírez, Salvador. *Stories for Carmencita*. Tr. Aloysius C. Gahan. Brooklyn, N.Y.: Brooklyn Daily Eagle Pr., 1914. 171 p. illus.*

Trans. of *Cuentos para mi Carmencita* (1915).

A collection of 29 stories, some of which are more like essays.

Peru

256. García Calderón, Ventura. *The white llama; being 'La venganza del cóndor' of Ventura García Calderón.* Tr. Richard Phibbs. London: The Golden Cockerel Pr., 1938. 123 p. illus.

A trans. of 21 stories from *La venganza del cóndor* (1924).

García Calderón's stylized view of the Peruvian Andes and his rather negative portrayal of the Indian caused a strong reaction by subsequent Peruvian writers who strived to present a more authentic picture of life in that region.

257. Palma, Ricardo. *The knights of the cape and thirty-seven other selections from the 'Tradiciones peruanas'.* Ed., tr. and intro. Harriet de Onís. Foreword José Rollín de la Torre-Bueno y Thorne. New York: Knopf, 1945. xvi, 246 p. bibliog. glossary*

Includes 38 selected stories from different volumes of Palma's *Tradiciones peruanas* (1872-1883, 1889-1911), a delightful blend of fiction, essay, and history.

Bibliography of *Tradiciones peruanas* (p. 241) and glossary of Spanish and Peruvian terms (pp. 243-246).

258. Valdelomar, Abraham. *Our children of the Sun (Los hijos del Sol); a suite of Inca legends from Peru.* Tr. and intro. Merritt Moore Thompson. Foreword J. Cary Davis. Carbondale, Illinois: Southern Illinois Univ. Pr., 1968. xiv, 94 p.

Trans. of *Los hijos del sol; cuentos incaicos* (1921).

An authorized trans. of 8 stories inspired by Inca legends. Not a scholarly rendition of Indian oral tradition, but creative prose by one of Peru's most important short story writers of the first part of the twentieth century.

Puerto Rico

259. Blanco, Tomás. *Los aguinaldos del Infante; glosa de Epifanía. The child's gifts; a Twelfth Night tale.* Tr. Harriet de Onís. San Juan: Pan American Book Co., 1954. 31 p. illus. musical score (rpt. San Juan: Pava Prints, 1962. 33 p.)

Bilingual edition of the Christmas story as narrated by Tomás Blanco. Beautifully illustrated.

260. Rodríguez Escudero, Néstor A. *Litoral: Short stories of the sea of Puerto Rico.* Tr. Louise Florea Sweetman. Prol. Federico de Onís. New York: Vantage Pr., 1969. xi, 138 p.*

Tr. of *Litoral; cuentos del mar de Puerto Rico* (1965), a collection of 28 stories.

261. Soto, Pedro Juan. *Spiks.* Tr. and intro. Victoria Ortiz. New York-London: Monthly Review Pr., 1973. 92 p.

Trans. of *Spiks* (1956), 13 short stories of Puerto Ricans living in New York. Soto is one of the leading writers of the generation of 1940 in Puerto Rico.

262. Tapia y Rivera, Alejandro. *Enardo and Rosael; an allegorical* *novella.* Tr. Alejandro Tapia, Jr. *et al.* Pref. Alejandro Tapia. New York: Philosophical Library, 1952. xix, 56 p.*

Trans. of *Enardo y Rosael, o el Amor a través de los siglos* (1872).

Uruguay

263. Quiroga, Horacio. *South American jungle tales.* Tr. Arthur Livingston. New York: Duffield, 1922. 166 p. illus. (rpt. London: Methuen, 1923; rpt. New York: Dodd-Mead, 1950)*

Trans. of *Cuentos de la selva* (1918) by one of Latin America's most talented short story writers. The 8 stories are set in the jungle forest region of Uruguay and Argentina.

3. Poetry

Argentina

264. Borges, Jorge Luis. *In praise of darkness.* Tr. Norman Thomas di Giovanni. Pref. Jorge Luis Borges. New York: E. P. Dutton, 1974. 142 p. (Toronto: Clark, Irwin, 1974)

A trans. of the 2nd ed. of *Elogio de la sombra* (1969), with some departures from the original text. Includes a bilingual presentation of the poems (parallel texts) with the addition of one poem from *Selected poems* (see No. 265). Also contains 6 prose selections translated by Di Giovanni with the collaboration of the author.

The preface originally appeared in *TriQuarterly.* The appendix also includes the original preface (in Spanish) to the first ed. of *Elogio de la sombra* (1969), notes on the text, notes on the translation, and a bibliographical note. An excellent edition.

It is noteworthy that for the English editions of his poetry Borges has again revised some of the original versions of his poems. Important changes are documented.

265. _____. *Selected poems, 1923-1967.* Ed. and intro. Norman Thomas di Giovanni. New York: Delacorte Pr., 1972. xxviii, 328 p. (London: Allen Lane, 1972. xxvi, 348 p.; rpt. New York: Delta, 1973. paper)

Twelve translators. Bilingual edition (parallel texts).

An especially prepared and revised edition of earlier translations, with revised texts in the original Spanish as well. Ninety poems, most of which are from *El otro, el mismo* (The self and the other). Poems are from the following collections: *Fervor de Buenos Aires* (1923), *Luna de enfrente* (1925), *Cuaderno San Martín* (1929), *El otro, el mismo* (1969), *Para las seis cuerdas* (1965), and *Museo* (1964).

Of special importance is the appendix, which includes the following sections: "New and unreprinted poems," "Prose pieces from *El Hacedor,*" "Prefaces and a dedication," "Supplement of 1969 revisions." Final pages of the volume contain the following divisions: "Notes," "Contents of principal editions of Borges' poetry," and an "Index of Spanish and English titles." (Pagination of American and British editions does not coincide.)

Included in this anthology is the poem "Deathwatch on the outside" ("La noche que en el Sur lo velaron"), tr. Robert Fitzgerald. It was publsihed separately in English trans. only by Grolier Book Shop (Cambridge, Mass., 1968).

266. Campo, Estanislao del. *Faust.* Tr. and intro. Walter Owen. Buenos Aires, 1943. xiii, 104 p.

Trans. of *Fausto* (1886), a visit to the city as narrated by an Argentine gaucho. The English translation was privately printed by the translator.

267. Hernández, José. *A fragment from 'Martín Fierro' (El gaucho).* Tr. Joseph Auslander. New York: Hispanic Society of America, 1932. (13) p.*

A verse trans. of the first 26 stanzas of the classic gauchesque poem (Part 1, 1872). The 2nd part was not published until 1879.

268. _____. *The gaucho Martín Fierro.* Tr. Frank Carrino, Alberto Carlos, and Norman Mangouni. Intro. Frank Carrino. Del Mar, N.Y.: Scholar's Facsimiles and Reprints, 1974. 99 p.; 78 p. bibliog. cloth.

A new English trans. of Part 1 of the poem (The flight) with notes on the text and a bibliography (pp. 1-99). As a separate section of the book, and with separate pagination, is a facsimile reproduction of the 1872 edition of *El gaucho Martín Fierro* (pp. 1-65) and the Spanish text of *Camino trasandino* (pp. 69-78) by the author. Actually two books in one volume.
The English translation forms a part of the UNESCO Collection of Representative Works of Latin American Literature. (For the paperback edition, see No. 269).

269. _____. *The gaucho Martín Fierro.* Tr. Frank Carrino, Alberto Carlos, and Norman Mangouni. Intro. Frank Carrino. Albany, N.Y.: State Univ. of New York Pr., 1974. 99 p. paper

Paperback edition of the English translation only of No. 268. Not a bilingual text.

270. _____. *The gaucho Martín Fierro.* Ed., adapted, tr., and intro. Walter Owen. Oxford: Basil Blackwell, 1935. xxiv, 326 p. illus. (rpt. New York: Farrar and Rinehart 1936; rpt. Buenos Aires: Editorial Pampa, 1960. 328 p.)

A rhymed verse translation, with very informative notes which explain customs, regional vocabulary, and other aspects of gaucho life.

271. _____. *El gaucho Martín Fierro. The gaucho Martín Fierro.* Tr. C. E. Ward. Annotated and rev. Frank G. Carrino and Alberto J. Carlos. Intro. Carlos Alberto Astiz. Albany, N.Y.: State Univ. of New York Pr. (Center for Inter-American Studies), 1967. xvii, 507 p. bibliog. illus.

A bilingual edition of the poem and the introduction. The trans. maintains the regional flavor of the original Spanish. Not a rhymed translation. Abundantly annotated, with a bibliography (pp. 506-507).

272. _____. *Martín Fierro.* Ed. and intro. Félix Coluccio. Buenos Aires: Cidegraf Argentina, 1969. 467 p. bibliog. illus.

A collector's item. The volume includes the original text of the poem *El gaucho Martín Fierro* (1872, 1879), an Italian trans. by Folco Testena (1935), the English trans. by Walter Owen (1935, see No. 270), and the French trans. by Paul Verdevoye (1965). Includes beautiful color illustrations.

273. Hernández, José. *Martín Fierro: An epic of the Argentine.* Ed., tr. and intro. Henry Alfred Holmes. New York Hispanic Institute of the United States, 1923. 185 p. (rpt. as *Martín Fierro, the Argentine gaucho epic,* and with a new intro., 1948. xxxvi, 193 p. illus.)*

Holmes' prose translation of the poem is annotated.

274. Pasamanik, Luisa. *The exiled angel.* Tr. Jack Hirschman. Los Angeles and Fairfax, California: Red Hill Pr., 1973. 1 vol. unpaged [19 p.]

Trans. of *El ángel desterrado* (1962), a poem in 22 sections.

275. Vallini, Alfredo. *Romances to the Argentine children.* Tr. Edith Rusconi Kaltovich. Charleston, Illinois: Prairie Poet Books, 1974. 26 p. illus. paper

Contains 21 *romances;* sensitive, simple poems about nature and people.

Chile

276. Alegría, Fernando. *Instructions for undressing the human race. Instrucciones para desnudar a la raza humana.* Tr. Lennart Bruce and Matthew Zion. San Francisco: Kayak Pr., 1968. 1 vol. unpaged [48 p.] illus.

Contemporary poems of social concern by noted critic and fiction writer.

277. _____. *Ten pastoral psalms.* Tr. Bernardo García and Matthew Zion. San Francisco: Kayak Pr., 1967. 1 vol. unpaged [27 p.] illus.*

Erotic poems with a few short prose selections.

278. Díaz Casanueva, Humberto. *Réquiem.* Tr. Angel Flores. Santiago de Chile: Ediciones del Grupo Fuego de la Poesía, 1958. 57 p.

A bilingual edition of the poems of *Réquiem* (1945). Díaz Casanueva writes poems of the nocturnal, irrational side of his being, but in an objective, contemplative manner.

279. Ercilla y Zúñiga, Alonso de. *La Araucana; the epic of Chile.* Adapted, tr. and intro. Walter Owen. Buenos Aires, 1945. lxix, 51 p.

Privately printed by the translator.

A trans. of Canto I of the famous epic poem of the conflict between the Spanish conquerors and the Araucanian Indians in Chile. This was planned to be the first volume of ten (Cantos I-XV), but the other volumes were not published. Text is based on the Salamanca edition (1574) with a few exceptions and additions. Changes in the text are annotated.

Ercilla actually was born in Madrid, and lived most of his life in Spain, but is often referred to as a poet of Chile due to the setting of his epic poem.

280. _____. *The Araucaniad: A version in English poetry of Alonso de Ercilla y Zúñiga's 'La Araucana'.* Tr.

and intro. Charles Maxwell Lancaster and Paul Thomas Manchester. Nashville, Tennessee: Vanderbilt Univ. Pr., 1945. 326 p.*

A scholarly edition of the translated epic poem which includes the original prologue by Ercilla y Zúñiga.

281. Ercilla y Zúñiga, Alonso de. *The historie of Aravcana; written in verse by Don Alonso de Ercilla translated out of the Spanische into Englishe prose allmost to the ende of the 16: canto.* Tr. George Carew. Transcribed and intro. Frank Pierce. Manchester, England: Univ. of Manchester Pr., 1964. xxi, 52 p.

A scholarly transcription of the oldest known English translation of Ercilla, a revised and edited version of the poem in the handwriting of George Carew (1555-1629). The manuscript (Lambeth Palace Library, ms 688) is based on the Spanish edition of Antwerp (1586).

Cantos 1-15 comprise the first part of the poem, so the translation ends at the beginning of the second part. The manuscript is carefully edited by Mr. Pierce.

282. Huidobro, Vicente. *Arctic poems.* Tr. William Witherup. Austin, Texas: Desert Review Pr., 1974. 88 p.

Trans. of *Poemas árticos* (1918), by one of the recognized leaders of avant-garde poetry in Spanish and self-proclaimed champion of Creationism.

283. Lihn, Enrique. *This endless malice; twenty-five poems.* Tr. Serge Echeverría and William Witherup. Northwood Narrows, N.H.: Lillabulero Pr., 1969. 83 p.*

A bilingual edition of poems from *La pieza oscura* (1963) and *Poesía de paso* (1966). Lihn is one of Chile's most promising poets of recent years.

284. Mistral, Gabriela [Lucila Godoy Alcayaga]. *Selected poems of Gabriela Mistral.* Ed. and tr. Doris Dana. Foreword Francisco Aguilera. Intro. Margaret Bates. Baltimore: Johns Hopkins Univ. Pr., 1971. xxix, 235 p. illus.*

A beautifully illustrated bilingual edition of poems from the Aguilar edition of her *Obras completas* (1958). Most of the poems had not previously been translated into English.

Selections are from: *Desolación* (1922), *Ternura* (1924), *Tala* (1938), *Lagar* (1954), and other collections.

Gabriela Mistral was the first Latin American to win the Nobel Prize for Literature (1945).

An "Index of themes" (pp. 233-235) completes the volume.

285. _____. *Selected poems of Gabriela Mistral.* Tr. and intro. Langston Hughes. Bloomington, Indiana: Indiana Univ. Pr., 1957. 119 p.

A representative collection of 74 poems arranged by theme. Selected from the following collections: *Desolación* (1922), *Tala* (1938), *Ternura* (1924), *Lagar* (1954) and *Lecturas para mujeres* (1923).

Included as a foreword is her Nobel Prize Citation by H. Gullberg of the Swedish Academy (pp. 13-16).

286. Neruda, Pablo [Neftalí Ricardo Reyes]. *Alturas de Macchu Picchu. The heights of Macchu Picchu.* Tr. Nathaniel Tarn. Pref. Robert Pring-

Mill. New York: Farrar, Straus and Giroux, 1967. xix, 71 p. (rpt. New York: Noonday Pr., 1967. paper). Originally published with title in reverse order. *The heights of Macchu Picchu. Alturas de Macchu Picchu.* London: Cape, 1966. 47 p. (rpt. 1972, paper)

A bilingual edition of this long poem from *Canto general* (1950). It reveals not only the poet of the surrealist *Residencias,* but the strongly committed writer for social and political justice. Neruda received the Nobel Prize for Literature in 1971, and with Borges is most widely translated into the English language.

287. Neruda, Pablo [Nefalí Ricardo Reyes]. *Bestiary. Bestiario.* Tr. Elsa Neuberger. Intro. Angel Flores. New York: Harcourt, Brace and World, 1965. 1 vol. unpaged [40 p.] illus. (rpt. New York: Harcourt, Brace and Jovanovich, 1974. paper)

Bilingual edition of *Bestiario,* first published in *Estravagario* (1958). A beautifully illustrated edition (woodcuts), first published as a collector's item with 300 autographed copies. The paperback edition does not include the woodcuts.

288. _____. *The Captain's verses. (Los versos del Capitán).* Tr. and imtro. Donald D. Walsh. New Directions, 1972. (viii), 151 p.

A well translated, bilingual edition of the 42 poems of *Los versos del Capitán* (1953).

289. _____. *The early poems.* Tr. Carlos B. Hagen and David Ossman. New York: New Rivers Pr., 1969. 100 p. illus.*

Includes 52 translations from the early collections: *Crepusculario* (1923), *El hondero entusiasta* (1923, © 1933), *20 poemas de amor y una canción desesperada* (1924), *Anillos* (1926), with 4 uncollected poems written before 1923.

This volume contains an afterword by Hagen (pp. 92-94) and his notes to the poems (pp. 95-98).

290. _____. *The elementary odes of Pablo Neruda.* Tr. Carlos Lozano. Intro. Fernando Alegría. New York: Las Americas, 191. 155 p.*

A bilingual collection of 21 odes from *Odas elementales* (1954), *Nuevas odas elementales* (1956), and *Tercer libro de las odas* (1957). The intro. (pp. 9-17) traces the thematic development of the odes.

291. _____. *Estravagaria.* Tr. Alistair Reid. London: Jonathan Cape, 1972. 303 p. (rpt. New York: Farrar, Straus and Giroux, 1974)

Bilingual edition of the 62 poems of *Estravagario* (1958). Parallel texts of originals and revised translations.

292. _____. *Five Decades: A selection (poems: 1925-1970).* Ed., tr. and pref. Ben Belitt. New York: Grove Pr., 1974. xxii, 431. bibliog.

A bilingual collection of 138 poems from 21 works, including 30 new translations never before published. Poems chosen from the following collections: *Residencia en la Tierra, I* (1925-1931), *II* (1931-1935), and *III* (1935-1945), *Canto general* (1950), *Odas elementales* (1954), *Nuevas odas elementales* (1956), *Tercer libro de las odas* (1957), *Navegaciones y regresos* (1959), *Estravagario* (1958), *Cien sonetos de amor* (1960), *Las piedras de Chile* (1960), *Cantos ceremoniales* (1961), *Plenos poderes* (1962), *Memorial de Isla Negra* (1964), *La barcarola* (1967), *Las manos del día* (1968), *Fin de mundo* (1969), and *Las piedras del cielo* (1970).

Poems from 1964 to 1970 are stressed. Neruda's essay, "Toward an impure poetry" (pp. xxi-xxii) is included, with a selected bibliography (pp. 429-431).

293. Neruda, Pablo [Neftalí Ricardo Reyes]. *Let the railsplitter awake, and other poems.* Intro. [Samuel Sillén]. Pref. [Pablo Neruda]. New York: Masses and Mainstream, 1950. 95 p.*

The preface by Neruda is in prose and is entitled "Our duty toward life" (tr. Joseph M. Bernstein, pp. 9-18).

Translations by 5 translators of 7 poems, all of which reflect the author's concern for the oppressed and his solidarity with the poor.

294. _____. *A new decade (poems: 1958-1967).* Ed. and intro. Ben Belitt. Tr. Ben Belitt and Alistair Reid. New York: Grove Pr., 1969. xlvi, 274 p. bibliog. (rpt. 1971, paper)

A bilingual collection of 113 poems from 7 works, with a selected bibliography (pp. 273-274). Selections are from: *Estravagario* (1958), *Cien sonetos de amor* (1959), *Las piedras de Chile* (1961), *Cantos ceremoniales* (1961), *Plenos poderes* (1962), *Memorial de Isla Negra* (1964), *La barcarola* (1967).

The intro. is a full length article:

"Pablo Neruda: A new decade" (pp. ix-xlvi).

295. _____. *New poems (1968-1970).* Ed., tr. and intro. Ben Belitt. New York: Grove Pr., 1972. xxxii, 153 p.

Another bilingual anthology with bibliographical references. Contains 59 poems from 3 collections: *Las manos del día* (1968), *Fin de mundo* (1969), and *Las piedras del cielo* (1970).

Of interest is the intro., "The moving finger and the unknown Neruda" (pp. xiii-xxxii).

296. _____. *Peace for twilights to come!* Tr. [Waldeen]. Bombay: Jayant Bhatt for People's Publishing House, 1950. 46 p. illus.

Trans. by "Waldeen" of "Que despierte el leñador" (In *Canto general,* 1950) which is also the cover title poem translation of *Let the railsplitter awake, and other poems* (see No. 293).

297. _____. *Residence on Earth.* Tr. Clayton Eshleman. San Francisco: Amber House Pr., 1962. 1 vol. unpaged [60 p.]*

Includes 9 selections from *Residencia en la Tierra,* I (1925-1931) and 15 poems from *Residencia en la Tierra,* II (1931-1935).

As an afterword or epilogue the translator includes "Pecho de pan," his own account of his experiences in translating the poems of the *Residencias.*

298. Neruda, Pablo [Neftalí Ricardo Reyes]. *Residence on Earth. Residencia en la Tierra.* Tr. and intro. Donald D. Walsh. New York: New Directions, 1973. xiv, 359 p.

A faithful trans. and bilingual edition of all the poems (115) of the three volumes of *Residencias:* I (1925-1931), II (1931-1935), and III (1935-1945). Based on the Losada (Buenos Aires) editions of 1958, 1961, and 1962 respectively.

This is the first edition of the complete *Residencias* in English translation.

299. _____. *Residence on Earth and other poems.* Ed. and tr. Angel Flores. Norfolk, Conn.: New Directions, 1946. 205 p. (rpt. New York: Gordian Pr., 1974)

A bilingual selection of 55 poems from the 3 volumes of *Residencias* (1925-1945), "recent poems" (1937-1944), and the yet unpublished volume "Canto general de Chile" (changed to *Canto general,* 1950).

300. _____. *Selected poems by Pablo Neruda.* Tr. Angel Flores. [New York], 1944. 26 p.*

Privately printed by the translator. Only 100 copies. A selection of 17 poems from *Residencia en la Tierra* (I and II) and *España en el corazón* (1936-1937), with 6 additional poems. This very limited edition is superseded by Flores' edition *Residence on Earth and other poems.* See No. 299.

301. _____. *Selected poems of Pablo Neruda.* Ed., tr. and foreword Ben Belitt. Intro. Luis Monguió. New York: Grove Pr., 1961. 320 p. bibliog. (rpt. 1963, paper)

A bilingual selection of 72 poems from the following works: *Residencia en la Tierra,* I (1925-1931), *Residencia en la Tierra,* II (1931-1935), *Tercera Residencia* (1935-1945), *Canto general* (1950), *Odas elementales* (1954), *Nuevas odas elementales* (1956), *Tercer libro de odas* (1957), *Navegaciones y regresos* (1959), *Estravagario* (1958).

Good intro. by Monguió (pp. 7-29) and informative essay by Belitt (pp. 30-38). The volume also contains Neruda's short essay, "Toward an impure poetry" (pp. 39-40).

A majority of the translations of this edition are included in *Five decades: A selection (poems: 1925-1970).* See No. 292. Selected bibliography, pp. 319-320.

302. _____. *Selected poems of Pablo Neruda.* Ed. Nathaniel Tarn. Tr. Anthony Kerrigan *et al.* London: Cape, 1970. xiii, 501 p. (rpt. New York: Delacorte Pr., 1972. 509 p.; rpt. New York: Delta, 1973, paper)

An excellent bilingual edition of 116 poems. Trans. by Anthony Kerrigan, W. S. Merwin, Alistair Reid, and Nathaniel Tarn. Based on the 2nd edition of his *Obras completas* (Buenos Aires: Losada, 1962).

Selections from the following works: *Veinte poemas de amor y una canción desesperada* (1924), *Residencia en la Tierra,* I (1933), *Residencia en la Tierra,* II (1935), *Tercera Residencia* (1947), *Canto general* (1950), *Odas elementales* (1954), *Nuevas odas elementales* (1956), *Estravagario* (1958), *Las piedras de Chile* (1961), *Cantos ceremoniales* (1961), *Plenos poderes* (1962), *Memorial de Isla Negra* (1964), *Una casa en la arena* (1966), and *La barcarola* (1967).

303. Neruda, Pablo [Ricardo Neftalí Reyes]. *Tres cantos materiales. Three material songs.* Tr. Angel Flores. New York: East River Editions, 1948. 1 vol. (unpaged) (31 p.) illus.*

Bilingual presentation of the three poems published in *Residencia en la Tierra,* II (1935). Only 200 copies printed.

304. _____. *Twenty love songs and a song of despair.* Tr. W. S. Merwin. London: Cape, 1969. 69 p. bibliog. (rpt. New York: Grossman, 1971)

Trans. of the poems of *Veinte poemas de amor y una canción desesperada* (1924), the collection that first won a reputation for Neruda as a young poet. A bilingual edition.
Included are two short bibliographies: ''Selected Bibliography'' (pp. 66-67) and ''Some translations of Pablo Neruda'' (pp. 67-68).

305. _____. *Twenty poems of Pablo Neruda.* Tr. James Wright and Robert Bly. Intro. Robert Bly. Madison, Minnesota: Sixties Pr., 1968, © 1967. 111 p.* (rpt. London: Rapp and Whiting, 1968)

A bilingual edition of poems from *Residencia en la Tierra,* I and II (1925-1935), *Canto general* (1950), and *Odas elementales* (1954-1957).
Bly's intro. is entitled ''Refusing to be Theocritus'' (pp. 7-17). Also included is the trans. of an interview by Bly with Neruda in July, 1966: ''The lamb and the pine cone'' (pp. 102-110).

306. _____. *We are many.* Tr. Alistair Reid. London: Cape Goliard,

1967. 1 vol. unpaged [32 p.] photos. (rpt. New York: Grossman, 1968; rpt. London: Cape, 1972 without photos)

A brief collection and bilingual edition of 9 poems from *Estravagario* (1958) and other works. The title suggests the strength of the working class.

307. _____ and César Vallejo [Peru]. *Neruda and Vallejo: Selected poems.* Ed. Robert Bly. Tr. Robert Bly, John Knoepfle, and James Wright. Boston: Beacon Pr., 1971. xiv, 269 p. (Toronto: Saunders of Toronto, 1971)

Bilingual edition, parallel texts. A revised and expanded format of the translations of Neruda and Vallejo published by The Sixties Pr.
As an intro. to the poetry of Neruda the essay by Bly, ''Refusing to be Theocritus'' (pp. 3-15) is reprinted. Short essays also precede the poems of Vallejo: ''What if after so many wings of birds'' (Bly, pp. 169-174) and ''Thoughts on César Vallejo'' (Knoepfle, pp. 175-176). The Neruda interview with Bly, ''The lamb and the pine cone'' (pp. 156-164) is reprinted also.
The 36 poems by Neruda are from the following collections: *Veinte poemas y una canción desesperada* (1924), *Residencia en la Tierra,* I and II (1933, 1935), *Tercera Residencia* (1947), *Canto general* (1950), and *Odas elementales* (1954).
The 38 Vallejo selections are from: *Los heraldos negros* (1918), *Trilce* (1922), *Poemas humanos* (1939), *España, aparta de mí este cáliz* (1939), and other works.

308. Oña, Pedro de. *Arauco tamed.*

Ed., tr. and intro. Charles Maxwell Lancaster and Paul Thomas Manchester. Albuquerque, N.M.: Univ. of New Mexico Pr., 1948. 283 p.*

A verse translation (in pentameter) of *Arauco domado* (1596), Oña's epic poem of the struggle between the Spaniards and the Araucanians of Chile. A scholarly edition.
Oña (1570-1643?) is the first native Chilean to achieve literary distinction.

309. Parra, Nicanor. *Anti-poems.* Tr. Jorge Elliott. San Francisco: City Lights Books, 1960. 32 p.*

Includes 13 poems from *Poemas y antipoemas* (1954). This volume may be seen as a brief introduction to the so-called "anti-poetry" of Parra.

310. _____. *Emergency poems.* Tr. Miller Williams. New York: New Directions, 1972. vi, 154 p.

A bilingual edition of 60 poems, with indices of Spanish titles and first lines (pp. 148-151) and their English equivalents (pp. 151-154). Parra is considered to be one of the most important poets in Latin America today.

311. _____. *Poems and antipoems.* Ed. and intro. Miller Williams. New York: New Directions, 1967. ix, 149 p. (rpt. London: Cape, 1968. 125 p.)

A bilingual edition of 56 poems from 4 collections, by 10 translators. Selections are from: *Poemas y antipoemas* (1954), *Versos de salón* (1962), *Canciones rusas* (1964), *Ejercicios respiratorios* (1966).

312. Piwonka, María Elvira. *Selected poems.* Tr. Edward Newman Horn. New York: Osmar Pr., 1967. 61 p.*

Contains 29 love poems. Translations are based on readings by the poet. Some of the poems may have been originally written in English or French.

313. Vicuña, Cecilia. *Sabor a mí.* Tr. Felipe Ehrenberg and Bill Lundberg. Cullompton, England: Beau Geste Pr., 1973. 148 p. illus.

A bilingual edition of poems by poet-artist Vicuña. A limited printing of only 250 copies.

Colombia

314. Ortiz-Vargas, Alfredo. *The towers of Manhattan: A Spanish American poet looks at New York.* Tr. Quincy Guy Burris. Albuquerque, N.M.: Univ. of New Mexico Pr., 1944. 137 p.

English trans. of *Las torres de Manhattan* (Boston, 1939). A brief biographical note is included (p. 137).

315. Silva, José Asunción. *A citizen of twilight.* Ed. and tr. G. G. King. New York: Longmans, Green, 1921. 38 p.*

Translations of 6 poems by the celebrated modernist are preceded by an introductory essay about the life and works of the poet.

Cuba

316. Giraudier, Antonio. *Green against linen, and other poems.* Tr. Antonio Giraudier and Samuel Weisberg. New York: Bookman Associates, 1957. 89 p.*

A bilingual selection of 63 poems. Poet-artist Giraudier has also written several illustrated books of poems in English. They do not list a translator, and since the poet speaks several languages, they were probably written originally in English.

317. González del Valle Ríos, Antolín. *Pregones de Villaclara.* Tr. Mary D. Bellamy. Miami: Fundación Educacional Latino-Americana, 1971. xii, 19 p. illus.*

A bilingual edition of *Pregones de Villaclara* (1939), prose poems which are memories of the street vendors of the poet's hometown. The English version follows the Spanish original (pp. 9-19).

318. Guillén, Nicolás. *Cuba libre; poems.* Tr. Langston Hughes and Ben Frederic Caruthers. Intro. Ben F. Caruthers. Los Angeles: Anderson-Ritchie (The Ward Ritchie Pr.), 1948. xi, 98 p. illus.*

Includes 50 selections from *El son entero* (1947). Many of the translations are composed in the Afro-American dialect in efforts to better reveal the nature of Cuba's famous Afro-Cuban poet.

319. _____. *Man-making words: Selected poems of Nicolás Guillén.* Ed., tr. and intro. Roberto Márquez and David Arthur McMurray. Amherst, Mass.: Univ. of Massachusetts Pr., 1972. xx, 214 p. glossary.

A bilingual collection of 46 poems from 10 published works, and four previously unpublished poems. A very useful section of notes and a glossary of Spanish terms is included (pp. 193-213).

Selections are from the following books: *Motivos de son* (1930), *Sóngoro consongo* (1931), *West Indies, Ltd.* (1934), *Canto para soldados y sones para turistas* (1937), *El son entero* (1947), *La paloma de vuelo popular* (1958), *Elegías* (1958), *Tengo* (1964), *Poemas de amor* (1964), *Poemas para el Che.*
Guillén combines the talent of a good poet with a strong sense of social and political commitment.

320. _____. *¡Patria o muerte! The great zoo and other poems.* Ed., tr. and intro. Roberto Márquez. New York-London: Monthly Review Pr., 1972. 223 p.

A bilingual edition of 39 poems of *El gran zoo* (1967) and 33 poems written between 1925 and 1969. All of the collections represented in *Man-making words* (see No. 319) are included in this volume, and with only two exceptions, the poems are different. Thus the works complement each other and provide an excellent source of Guillén's work.

321. _____. *Tengo.* Tr. Richard Carr. Detroit: Broadside Pr.. 1974.

Trans. of the poems of *Tengo* (1964).

322. Heredia [y Campuzano], José María. *Selections from the poems of Don José María Heredia; with translations of English verse.* Tr. and pref. James Kennedy. Havana: Imprenta de José María Eleizegui, 1844. 32 p.

A bilingual edition of 5 poems, including a translation by Heredia of "Written in an album" by Lord Byron. See No. 555.

323. Padilla, Heberto. *Sent off the field; a selection from the poetry of Heberto Padilla.* Tr. J[ohn] M[ichael] Cohen. London: Deutsch, 1972. 127 p.

Selections from *El justo tiempo humano* (1970), *Fuera del juego* (1969), and subsequently written unpublished poems.
Padilla, a prize-winning poet of Revolutionary Cuba, was the center of controversy after the publication of *Fuera del juego,* a work deemed anti-revolutionary by many of his compatriots.

324. _____. *Subversive poetry: The Padilla affair.* Tr. F. Calzón *et al.* Intro. Laura Pérez. Washington, D.C.: Georgetown Univ. Cuban Students Assoc., (1972). 1 vol. unpaged [47 p.] paper*

Various translators. A bilingual selection of 15 poems from *Fuera del juego* (1969). The intro. is critical of the Castro regime.

Dominican Republic

325. Fiallo, Fabio. *Poems of the little girl in heaven.* Tr. Margaret B. Hurley. Ciudad Trujillo, 1937. 69 p.

(original title: *Poemas de la niña que está en el cielo,* 1935)
Delicate prose poems.

Ecuador

326, Carrera Andrade, Jorge. *País secreto. Secret Country.* Tr. Muna Lee [de Muñoz Marín]. Intro. John Peale Bishop. New York: Macmillan, 1946. xvii, 77 p.*

A bilingual edition of the poems of *País secreto* (1940) and other poems. Total of 30 poems by Ecuador's most noted twentieth-century poet.

327. _____. *Selected poems of Jorge Carrera Andrade.* Ed., tr. and intro. H[offman] R[eynolds] Hays. Albany, N.Y.: State Univ. of New York Pr., 1972. xxvi, 259 p.*

An anthology of 62 poems from 9 collections of poetry written between 1926 and 1966. Carrera Andrade is regarded as an excellent creator of brilliant metaphors and images. Poems are from the following collections: *La guirnalda del silencio* (1926), *Boletines de mar y tierra* (1928-1930), *Cuaderno de poemas indios* (1928), *El tiempo manual* (1935), *Lugar de origen* (1945-1947), *Familia de la noche* (1952-1953), *Hombre planetario* (1957-1963), *Crónica de las Indias* (1965) and *El alba llama a la puerta* (1965-1966).

328. _____. *To the Bay Bridge. Canto al puente de Oakland.* Tr. Eleanor L. Turnbull, Stanford, California: Stanford Univ. Pr. (Office of Pan American Relations; Hoover Library on War, Revolution and Peace), 1941. 20 p.*

A bilingual text.

329. _____. *Visitor of mist.* Tr. and intro. G. R. Coulthard. London: Williams and Norgate, 1950. 74 p.*

A collection of 44 poems, some of which are translated by Kathleen Nott. This edition complements the edition of *Secret Country.*

330. Cevallos Larrea, Cristóbal. *La gesta amazónica; con versión al inglés.* Tr. C. Victor Stahl. Riobamba, Ecuador: Imprenta "Pichincha," 1961. 16 p.

This bilingual edition of the short epic poem *La gesta amazónica* (1945) which tells of the exploits of Francisco de Orellana, discoverer of the Amazon River, includes notes and brief commentaries. The English version, "Tale of the Amazon," is written in iambic pentameter (pp. xi-xiv).

331. Donoso Pareja, Miguel. *Primera canción del exilado. The exile's first song.* Tr. Elinor Randall. México: Ediciones El Corno Emplumado, 1966. 64 p. illus.

The English version of the poem follows the original (pp. 37-64). This is a song directed to the exiled poet's homeland.

Guatemala

332. Castillo, Otto René. *Let's go! Vámonos patria a caminar.* Tr. and intro. Margaret Randall. London: Cape Goliard Pr., 1971. 1 vol. unpaged [85 p.]

A bilingual trans. of the 19 poems of *Vámonos patria a caminar* (1965), poetic works by a Guatemalan revolutionary who was killed in guerilla action. Poems of strong political and social commitment.

Mexico

333. Cruz, Sor Juana Inés de la [Juana de Asbaje y Ramírez de Santillana]. *The pathless grove: Sonnets of Sor Juana Inés de la Cruz, 1651-1695.* [Ed.], tr. and intro. Pauline Cook. Prairie City, Illinois: The Decker Pr., 1950. xviii, 55 p.*

By Mexico's outstanding Baroque poet.

A bilingual collection of 22 sonnets and "The pathless grove," an extract from "Respuesta a Sor Filotea" (pp. 48-53). This is her justification of her way of life. The prose selection is also in English with the Spanish original.

334. Gorostiza, José. *Muerte sin fin. Death without end.* Tr. and intro. Laura Villaseñor. Austin: Univ. of Texas Pr. (Humanities Research Center), 1969. 39 p. bibliog. illus.

A nicely annotated bilingual edition of *Muerte sin fin* (1952), with a selected bibliography (pp. 35-39).

335. Nervo, Amado. *Confessions of a modern poet.* Ed. and tr. Dorothy M. Kress. Boston: Bruce Humphries, 1935. 50 p.*

Contains "Confessions of a modern poet," a prose selection about a love affair.

Also included are 20 poems, mostly from *La amada inmóvil* (1922). Modernist love poetry.

336. Novo, Salvador. *Nuevo amor.* Tr. Edna Worthley Underwood. Portland, Maine: The Mosher Pr., 1935. 1 vol. unpaged [52 p.]*

A collection of 10 selections, mostly from *Nuevo amor* (1933). Despite the Spanish title, it is not a bilingual edition. This is the first single volume in English translation dedicated to a Mexican poet.

337. Pacheco, José Emilio. *Tree between two walls.* Tr. Edward Dorn and Gordon Brotherston. Los Angeles: Black Sparrow Pr., 1969. 15 p.*

A trans. of "Arbol entre dos

muros," from the collection *Los elementos de la noche* (1963).

338. Paz, Octavio. *Configurations*. Tr. G. Aroul *et al*. Intro. Muriel Rukeyser. New York: New Directions, 1971. vi, 198 p. (rpt. London: Cape, 1971)

A bilingual edition of poems from 4 books: *Piedra de sol* (1957), *Blanco* (1967), and 34 selections from *Salamandra* (1962) and *Ladera este* (1969).
"Blanco" is an experimental poem which may be read and interpreted in many different ways.

339. _____. *Early poems, 1935-1955*. Tr. Muriel Rukeyser *et al*. New York: New Directions, 1973. 145 p. paper (rpt. Bloomington, Indiana: Indiana Univ. Pr., 1974. cloth)

A revised edition of *Selected poems* (see No. 340) with a few deletions, additions, and the poet's own revision of the Spanish originals. Additions include work by several translators. Poems from one collection are added (*Estación violenta*, 1958). Some changes in the titles of poems have also been made by the author.
This bilingual edition contains 46 selections.

340. _____. *Selected poems of Octavio Paz*. Tr. and foreword Muriel Rukeyser. Bloomington, Indiana: Indiana Univ. Pr., 1963. 171 p.*

Of the UNESCO Collection of Representative Works of Latin American Literature.
A bilingual edition of 53 selections from 6 works which include: *Condición de nube, El girasol, Semillas*

para un himno (1954), *Piedras sueltas, Puerta condenada, A la orilla del mundo* (1942), and *La estación violenta* (1958). The volume also contains a trans. of the prologue to *Libertad bajo palabra* (1949, 2nd ed. 1960).
This is a good collection of poems which is superseded by *Early poems, 1935-1955*.

341. _____. *Piedra de sol. The sun stone*. Tr. Donald Gardner. York, England: Cosmos Publications, 1969. 31 p.

A bilingual edition (parallel texts) of *Piedra de sol* (1957). A limited edition of 750 copies.

342. _____. *Sun-stone*. Tr. Peter Miller. Toronto: Contact Pr., 1963. xii, 67 p.

A bilingual edition of *Piedra de sol* (1957).

343. _____. *Sun stone. Piedra de sol*. Tr. Muriel Rukeyser. New York: New Directions, 1963. 47 p.*

A bilingual text of the poem. It also appears in *Configurations* (see No. 338).

344. _____ *et al. Renga; a chain of poems*. Tr. Charles Tomlinsen. Intro. Octavio Paz. Foreword Claude Roy. New York: George Brazilier, 1972. 95 p.

A French edition of this polyglot poem was published in 1971. It may be read horizontally or vertically, or in other combinations. Texts in French, Italian, and Spanish include the parallel English translation.
The authors are: Paz (Spanish),

Jacques Roubaud (French), Edoardo Sanguineti (Italian), and Charles Tomlinsen (English).

Other essays are included by Jacques Roubaud and Charles Tomlinsen.

345. Torres Bodet, Jaime. *Selected poems.* Ed., tr. and intro. Sonja Karsen. Bloomington, Indiana: Indiana Univ. Pr., 1964. 155 pl. bibliog.*

A bilingual selection of 43 poems from 11 collections, which trace the poet's development from lyrical simplicity, to surrealism, and finally more structured, pensive poems.

Of the UNESCO Collection of Representative Works of Latin American Literature.

Poems are from the following works: *Fervor* (1918), *Canciones* (1922), *El corazón delirante* (1922), *Los días* (1923), *Poemas* (1924), *Biombo* (1925), *Destierro* (1930), *Cripta* (1937), *Sonetos* (1949), *Fronteras* (1954), *Sin tregua* (1957).

A useful bibliography completes the volume (pp. 153-155).

Nicaragua

346. Cardenal, Ernesto. *Homage to the American Indians.* Tr. Monique and Carlos Altschul. Baltimore: Johns Hopkins Univ. Pr., 1973. 116 p. illus. glossary

Trans. of the 17 poems of *Homenaje a los indios americanos* (1970), one of the principal collections by priest and poet-philosopher Cardenal, considered to be one of the most outstanding contemporary poets of Latin America.

Footnotes by the translators refer to words or phrases which appear in English in the Spanish language originals of the poems. Included is a glossary of Spanish and Indian terms (pp. 113-116). A beautifully arranged and illustrated edition.

347. _____. *Psalms of struggle and liberation.* Tr. Emile G. McAnany. Foreword Thomas Merton. New York: Herder and Herder, 1971. 76 p. photographs. (rpt. New York: Seabury Pr., 1973)

Trans. of the 25 poems of *Salmos* (1969), "psalms" dedicated to the poor and oppressed.

348. Cuadra, Pablo Antonio. *The jaguar & the moon. El jaguar y la luna.* Tr. and intro. Thomas Merton. Greensboro, N.C.: Unicorn Pr., 1974. 40 p.

Bilingual edition of 10 poems from *El jaguar y la luna* (1959). Includes a biographical sketch of the poet (pp. 37-38).

349. Darío, Rubén. *Eleven poems of Rubén Darío.* Tr. Thomas Walsh and Salomón de la Selva. Intro. Pedro Henríquez Ureña. New York-London: G. P. Putnam's Sons, 1916. ix, 49 p. bibliog.*

A brief anthology published for the Hispanic Society of America (Publication No. 105). A bilingual edition of poems by the most important modernist poet and one of the greatest and most influential figures in the history of Hispanic poetry.

A bibliography of criticism of Darío's works compiled by Pedro Henríquez Ureña is also included (pp. 47-49).

350. Darío, Rubén. *Prosas profanas and other poems.* Tr. and pref. Charles B. McMichael. New York: Nicholas L. Brown, 1922. 60 p.*

A brief collection of 8 poems, 5 of them from *Prosas profanas* (1896). Includes a trans. of the original prologue by Darío of *Prosas profanas.*

351. _____. *Selected poems of Rubén Darío.* Tr. Lysander Kemp. Prol. Octavio Paz. Austin: Univ. of Texas Pr., 1965. 149 p. illus.

A bilingual collection which includes 74 poems from the following collections: *Abrojos* (1887), *Rimas* (1887), *Azul* (1888), *Prosas profanas y otros poemas* (1896), *Cantos de vida y esperanza* (1905), *Los cisnes y otros poemas* (1905), *El canto errante* (1907), *Poema del otoño y otros poemas* (1910), *Canto a la Argentina* (1914), and 8 miscellaneous poems.

The prologue by Paz is entitled "The seashell and the siren" (pp. 7-18). An epilogue in the form of a speech given by Pablo Neruda and Federico García Lorca to the PEN Club (Buenos Aires, 1933) is included (pp. 139-141), and the volume is complete with an index to titles in English and Spanish (pp. 145-149).

Peru

352. Chocano, José Santos. *Spirit of the Andes.* Ed., tr., and foreword Edna Worthley Underwood. Portland, Maine: The Mosher Pr., 1935. [xviii], 43 p.*

Selected poems from various collections of the famous modernist poet. This is the first English edition of his poetry.

353. Cisneros, Antonio. *The spider hangs too far from the ground.* Tr. Maureen Ahern, William Rowe and David Tipton. London: Cape Goliard Pr., 1970. 1 vol. unpaged [69 p.] (New York: Grossman, 1970)

A collection of 40 poems from *Comentarios reales* (1964), *Canto ceremonial contra un oso hormiguero* (1968), and *Crónica de Chapi* (1965).

354. Llona, Teresa María. *Intersection.* Tr. Marie Pope Wallis. Prol. Gabriela Mistral. Dallas, Texas: The Story Book Pr., 1950. ix, 64 p.*

Trans. of 45 poems from *Encrucijada* (1938). Llona revives the *romance,* the popular ballad, in poems of love. A constant theme is that of the martyrdom of womanhood.

355. Vallejo, César. *Poemas humanos. Human poems.* Tr. and foreword Clayton Eshleman. New York: Grove Pr., 1968. xxv, 326 p. (rpt. London: Cape, 1969).

A bilingual edition of this important collection (*Poemas humanos,* 1939) based on 5 editions of the work. Vallejo is considered to be one of the greatest and most influential post-modernist poets.

356. _____. *Spain, let this cup pass from me.* Tr. Alvaro Cardona-Hine. Fairfax, California: Red Hill Pr., 1972. 51 p. paper*

An admittedly awkward trans. of the poems of *España, aparta de mí este cáliz* (1939), written in reaction to the Spanish Civil War.

357. _____. *Spain, take this cup from me. España, aparta de mí este* *cáliz.* Tr. Clayton Eshelman and José Rubia Barcia. New York: Grove Pr., 1974. xiii, 77 p.

A bilingual edition of the 15 poems of the collection (1939). Ample notes on the text are included (pp. 72-77).

358. Vallejo, César. *Ten versions from 'Trilce'.* Tr. Charles Tomlinsen and Henry Gifford. Intro. Henry Gifford. Cerrillos, New Mexico: San Marcos Pr., 1970. 26 p. paper*

From *Trilce* (1922), Vallejo's most important collection.

359. _____. *Trilce.* Tr. and pref. David Smith. Intro. Fernando Alegría. Tokyo: Mushinsha, 1973. 213 p. illus. (rpt. New York: Grossman, 1974)

A bilingual edition of all the poems (77) from *Trilce* (1922). A very important contribution to the bibliography of Latin American literature in English translation.

360. _____. *Twenty poems of César Vallejo.* Ed. and tr. Robert Bly, John Knoepfle, and James Wright. Madison, Minnesota: Sixties Pr., 1963, © 1962. 63 p. illus.*

A selection of poems mostly from *Los heraldos negros* (1918), *Trilce* (1922), and *Poemas humanos* (1939).

361. _____ and Pablo Neruda. See No. 307.

Puerto Rico

362. Bauzá, Obdulio. *Selected poems.* Tr. Helen Wohl Patterson. Prol. Concha Meléndez. Madrid, 1961. 133 p.

A bilingual edition of 30 poems from 5 collections: *Las hogueras de cal* (1947), *La casa solariega* (1954), *Las voces esperadas* (1956), *La canción de los olivos* (1958), and *El libro de las nubes* (1959).

Prologue in Spanish only is entitled "Tiempo y recuerdo en la poesía de Obdulio Bauzá" (pp. 9-20).

363. Carrero, Jaime. *Aquí, los ángeles. Here, the angels.* Tr. and intro. Gilbert Neiman. San Germán, Puerto Rico: Universidad Interamericana, 1960, i, 11 p. illus.

The intro. is translated into Spanish by Carmen Rodríguez. Very short poems accompanied by the poet-painter's own illustrations.

364. Dávila, Virgilio. *Pueblito de antes.* Tr. José Antonio Dávila. San Juan, Puerto Rico: Editorial Cordillera, 1967. 99 p.

A bilingual edition of poetry.

365. Gil de Rubio, Víctor M. *Poemas puertorriqueños. Puerto Rican poems.* Barcelona: Ediciones Rumbos, 1968. 157 p.

A bilingual selection of poems.

Uruguay

366. Zorrilla de San Martín, Juan. *Tabaré: An Indian legend of Uruguay.* Tr. Walter Owen. Rev. ed. and tr. Frank P. Hebblewaite. Washington, D.C.: Pan American Union, 1956. xliii, 366 p.*

Of the UNESCO Collection of Representative Works of Latin American Literature. A bilingual edition of Zorrilla de San Martín's romantic epic *Tabaré* (1888).

This poem was earlier published as *Tabaré; an epic poem of the early days of Uruguay*. Tr. Ralph Walter Huntington. Buenos Aires, 1934. 174 p.

Venezuela

367. Bello, Andrés. *A georgic of the tropics. Silva a la agricultura de la zona tórrida*. Tr. John Cook Wyllie. Charlottesville, Virginia: King Lindsay Printing Corp., 1954. 39 p.*

Trans. of *Silva a la agricultura de la zona tórrida* (1826).
A bilingual edition of the neoclassic poem. Practically a literal translation. Bello's own notes from the original edition are included.

4. Drama

Argentina

368. Gorostiza, Carlos. *The bridge; a drama in two acts*. Tr. and adapted Louis L. Curcio. New York: Samuel French, 1961. 104 p. illus.*

(original title: *El puente,* 1949)
A play inspired by the author's memories of life in a residential district of Buenos Aires. A movie version of the play was released in 1951.

369. Leguizamón, Martiniano. *Calandria; a drama of gaucho life*. Tr. [Orosi]. New York: Hispanic Society of America, 1932. 65 p.*

(original title: *Calandria,* 1896)
A gaucho play. The protagonist redeems himself through hard work.

Chile

370. Marín, Juan. *Orestes and I; a play in three acts*. Tr. Richard P. Butrick. Tokyo: Asia-America Editors, 1940. 66 p.

(original title: *Orestes y yo*, 1940)
Adaptation of novel of the same title.

371. Neruda, Pablo [Nefalí Ricardo Reyes]. *Fulgor y muerte de Joaquín Murieta. The splendor and death of Joaquín Murieta*. Tr. and foreword Ben Belitt. Foreword Pablo Neruda. New York: Farrar, Straus and Giroux, 1972. xviii, 184 p. (Toronto: Doubleday Canada, 1972; rpt. London: Alcove Pr., 1973)

(original title: *Fulgor y muerte de Joaquín Murieta*, 1966)
A bilingual edition based on the text of Neruda's *Obras completas* (Buenos Aires: Losada, 1968).
Neruda calls the work a "play-song." The translator refers to it as a melodious pantomine, but at the same time a tragic work.

372. Wolff, Egon. *Paper flowers*. Tr. Margaret Sayers Peden. Columbia, Missouri: Univ. of Missouri Pr., 1971. 79 p.

(original title: *Flores de papel*, 1970)
A chamber play of the theme of his three-act drama *Los invasores* (The invaders). Only two characters.

Cuba

373. Gómez de Avellaneda, Gertrudis. *Belshazzar*. Tr. W. F. Burbank. London: B. F. Stevens and

Brown, 1914. 64 p. (San Francisco: A. M. Robertson, 1914)*

(original title: *Baltasar*, 1858)
A four-act play in verse of the love of two Hebrew captives in Babylon.

Guatemala

374. Solórzano, Carlos. *The hands of God.*Tr. Keith Leonard and Mario Soria. Hiram, Ohio: Hiram College Ibero-American Celebration, 1968. 38 p.*

(original title: *Las manos de Dios*, 1956)
A very modern work which focuses on man's struggle against conformity and spiritual enslavement.

Mexico

375. Carballido, Emilio. *The golden thread and other plays.* Tr. and intro. Margaret Sayers Peden. Austin: Univ. of Texas Pr., 1970. xvii, 237 p.

Six plays of successful dramatist and novelist Carballido, who offers his literary vision of reality and individual responsibility.
Translated plays are: *The mirror* (*El espejo*), *The time and the place* (*El lugar y la hora*, 1957), *The golden thread* (*La hebra de oro*, 1956), *The intermediate zone* (*La zona intermedia*, 1948), *The clockmaker from Córdoba* (*El relojero de Córdoba*, 1960), and *Theseus* (*Teseo*, 1962).

376. Orozco, R. Efrén. *El mensajero del sol* (bilingual text). México: Secretaría de Gobernacíon, 1941, 64 p.

377. Usigli, Rodolfo. *Another springtime; a drama in three acts.* Tr.

Wayne Wolfe. New York-London: Samuel French, 1961. 73 p. illus.*

(original title: *Otra primavera*, 1938)
About an old man thought to be mad, and his wife who attempts to cure his insanity.

378. _____. *Crown of shadows: an antihistorical play.* Tr. William F. Stirling. Prol. Rodolfo Usigli. London: A. Wingate, 1946. 100 p.

(original title: *Corona de sombra*, 1943)
One of Usigli's finest plays. Centers around the struggle between Juárez and Maximilian for sovereignty during the period of 1864 to 1867.

379. _____. *Two plays: Crown of light. One of these days. . . .* Tr. Thomas Bledsoe. Intro. Willis Knapp Jones. Foreword J. Cary Davis. Carbondale, Illinois: Southern Illinois Univ. Pr., 1971. 234 p.*

(original titles: *Corona de luz*, 1965, and *Un día de éstos*, 1955)
Corona de luz deals with the period of Mexican history between 1529 and 1531. The play analyzes the relationship between Christianity and paganism.
Un día de éstos considers the problem of correct procedures for electing the president.

Puerto Rico

380. Marqués, René. *The oxcart.* Tr. and abridged Charles Pilditch. New York: Scribner's, 1969. xiv, 155 p. illus.

(original title: *La carreta*, 1952)
Traces the move of a Puerto Rican family from the country to San Juan, then to New York. Social commentary.

Uruguay

381. Sánchez, Florencio. *Representative plays of Florencio Sánchez.* Ed and tr. Willis Knapp Jones. Rev. tr. Glenn Barr. Intro. Ruth Richardson. Washington D.C.: Pan American Union, 1961. 326 p. bibliog.*

Translations of 11 plays written between 1903 and 1907.

The plays are: *My son the lawyer* (*M'hijo el dotor*, 1904), *The immigrant girl* (*La gringa*, 1904), *Down the gully* (*Barranca abajo*, 1905), *Our children* (*Nuestros hijos*, 1907), *Midsummer Day parents* (*Cédulas de San Juan*, 1904), *The newspaper boy* (*Canillita*, 1904), *The healing hand* (*Mano santa*, 1905), *Evicted* (*El desalojo*, 1906), *The tigress* (*La tigra*, 1907), *Phony money* (*Moneda falsa*, 1907), *The family circle* (*En familia*, 1905).

Sánchez is known as Latin America's first modern dramatist. His plays emphasize social and cultural conflicts. A selected bibliography on the playwright is also included (pp. 13-14).

4. Essay*

Argentina

382. Borges, Jorge Luis, foreword. *The gaucho.* José Luis Lanuza. Tr. J. R. Wilcock. New York: Crown, 1968. 1 vol. [55 p.], unpaged, photos*

Borges' foreword (pp. 9-11) provides insight concerning the nature of the gaucho. The authorship of this collector's item has been erroneously attributed to Borges.

*A selected reading list. Preference is given to works by authors already included in this bibliography and to essay collections of significant literary quality. Works of a sociological or political nature, and essays of literary criticism, are generally excluded.

383. _____. *Other inquisitions, 1937-1952.* Tr. Ruth L. C. Simms. Intro. James E. Irby. Austin: Univ. of Texas Pr., 1964. xviii, 205 p. (rpt. New York: Washington Square Pr., 1966. paper; rpt. New York: Simon and Schuster, 1971. paper; rpt. London: Souvenir Pr., 1973)

(original title: *Otras inquisiciones*, 1952)

Contains 38 essays and an epilogue. Other works by Borges contain essays as well. See No. 222, No. 224.

384. Martínez Estrada, Ezequiel. *X-Ray of the pampa.* Tr. Alain Swietlicki. Intro. Thomas F. McGann. Austin: Univ. of Texas Pr., 1971. 415 p.

(original title: *Radiografía de la pampa*, 1933)

A severe, bitter vision of Argentine reality in 1930. Highly poetic, metaphorical prose of great impact.

385. Porchia, Antonio. *Voices.* Tr. W. S. Merwin. Chicago: Follet (Big Table Paperback), 1969. 64 p. illus. paper

(original title: *Voces*, 1943)
Aphorisms.

386. Sarmiento, Domingo Faustino. *Life in the Argentine Republic in the days of the tyrants; or civilization and barbarism.* Tr. and intro. Mrs. Horace Mann. New York: Hurd and Houghton, 1868. (rpt. New York: Hafner, 1960. xxxv, 400 p. paper; (rpt. New York: Macmillan, 1961. 288 p. paper)

(original title: *Civilización y barbarie: Vida de Juan Facundo Quiroga*, 1845)

Classic essay which establishes the theme of "Civilization vs. Barbarism" in Latin American letters. Juan Facundo Quiroga was one of dictator Rosas' *caudillos*. Book includes some excellent descriptive passages of the pampa.

387. Sarmiento, Domingo Faustino. *A Sarmiento anthology.* Ed. and intro. Allison Williams Bunkley. Tr. Stuart E. Grummon. Princeton, New Jersey: Princeton Univ. Pr., 1948. 336 p.* (London: Oxford Univ. Pr., 1948)

Selected writings by the famous nineteenth-century essayist and politician.

388. _____. *Sarmiento's travels in the United States in 1847.* Tr. and intro. Michael Aaron Rockland. Princeton, New Jersey: Princeton Univ. Pr., 1970. xiii, 330 p. plates

(from *Viajes por Europa, Africa y América*, 1849-1851)
Letters which reveal admiration for American culture and government. Acute observations.

389. _____. *Travels; a selection.* Tr. Inés Muñoz. Washington, D.C.: Pan American Union, 1963. 297 p. paper

(from *Viajes por Europa, Africa y America*, 1849-1851)
Selections of letters and essays written during his travels as a representative of the Chilean government. He later became Argentina's ambassador to the United States.

390. Ugarte, Manuel. *The destiny of a continent.* Ed. and intro J. F. Rippy. Tr. Catherine A. Phillips. New York: Knopf, 1925. xxi, 296 p. bibliog. (rpt. New York: AMS Pr., 1970)

(original title: *El destino de un continente*, 1923)

A strong critic of Yankee imperialism and outspoken defender (and critic) of Latin American culture, Ugarte also wrote works of poetry and fiction.

391. Vigil, Constancio C. *The fallow land (El erial).* Tr. Lawrence Smith. Foreword Willard L. Sperry. New York-London: Harper and Bros., 1946. 208 p.

(original title: *El erial*)
Philosophical reflections. Parables. 13 selections.

392. _____. *Seeds. . .; selections from the works of Constancio C. Virgil.* Tr. Nina Bull. [Intro.] Gaetano Massa. [Pref.] Nina Bull. Forest Hills, N.Y.: Las Americas, 1943, viii, 61 p.*

A collection of 24 essays, reflections, parables, and aphorisms from 4 works.

Chile

393. Serrano, Miguel. *El/Ella; book of magic love.* Tr. Frank MacShane. New York: Harper and Row, 1972. 75 p. (rpt. London: Routledge and Kegan Paul, 1973)

(original title unavailable)
A kind of fictionalized philosophy or philosophical prose.

394. _____. *The serpent of paradise; the story of an Indian pilgrimage.* Tr. Frank MacShane. London: Rider, 1963. 269 p. (Rev. ed. New York: Harper and Row, 1972. 184 p.)

(original title: *La serpiente del paraíso*, 1963)
The American edition has several sections deleted.
Philosophical reflections based on the author's visit to India. A spiritual pilgrimage.

395. Serrano, Miguel. *The ultimate flower*. Tr. Frank MacShane. London: Routledge and Kegan Paul, 1969. vi, 101 p. illus. (rpt. New York: Schocken Books, 1970. vi, 97 p. illus.)

(original title unavailable)
Fictionalized account of religious experience.

396. _____. *The visits of the Queen of Sheba*. Tr. Frank MacShane. Foreword C. G. Jung. Bombay-New York: Asia Publishing House, 1960. viii, 72 p. illus. (London: Asia Publishing House, 1961: 2nd ed. London: Routledge and Kegan Paul, 1972. xi, 61 p. illus.)

(original title: *Las visitas de la reina de Saba*, 1960)
Poetic revelation of the unconscious, of archetypes. Contains 16 poetic, philosophical essays.

Cuba

397. Martí, José. *The America of José Martí; selected writings of José Martí*. Ed. and tr. Juan de Onís. Intro. Federico de Onís. New York: Noonday Pr., 1953. xiii, 335 p. (rpt. New York: Funk and Wagnalls, 1968)

24 selections by modernist poet and essayist Martí.

Mexico

398. Beteta, Ramón. *Jarano*. Tr. John Upton. Austin: Univ. of Texas Pr., 1970. 163 p.

(original title: *Jarano*, 1966)
Beautifully written memoirs of boyhood in which the author recalls events of the Mexican Revolution.

399. González Obregón, Luis. *The streets of Mexico*. Tr. Blanche Collet Wagner. San Francisco: George Fields, 1937. 200 p.*

(original title: *Las calles de México*, 1924)
Contains 41 stories, legends, histories of Mexico City. Some of these essays border on fiction, like the *Tradiciones* of Peruvian Ricardo Palma.

400. Nervo, Amado. *Plenitude*. Tr. and intro. William F. Rice. Los Angeles: Jesse Ray Miller, 1928. 153 p.*

(original title: *Plenitud*, 1918)
A collection of 60 reflections in poetic prose.

401. Paz, Octavio. *¿Aguila o Sol? Eagle or Sun?* Tr. Eliot Weinberger. New York: October House, 1970. 125 p.*

(original title: *¿Aguila o Sol?*, 1951)
Bilingual edition of prose poems which give insight into the author's own search for identity as a poet. Composed of three sections: "Trabajos del poeta" (1949), "Arenas movedizas" (1949), and "¿Aguila o Sol?" (1949-1950). A few changes from the original text are made.

402. _____. *Alternating current*. Tr. Helen R. Lane. New York: Viking Pr., 1973. 215 p. (rpt. 1973. 213 p. paper)

(original title: *Corriente alterna*, 1967)
Contains 42 essays on literature and art, contemporary subjects, and political problems. Written during two periods: 1959-1961 and 1965-1967.

403. _____. *The bow and the lyre. (El arco y la lira)*. Tr. Ruth L. C. Simms. Intro. and two forewords Octavio Paz. Austin: Univ. of Texas Pr., 1973. xi, 281 p.

(original title: *El arco y la lira*, 1956)

Based on the 2nd edition of the work, 1967.

Essays mainly about the nature of poetry. Divided into four sections according to theme. A major work, and an important contribution to the bibliography in English of Mexico's leading poet and essayist.

404. Paz, Octavio. *Conjunctions and disjunctions.* Tr. Helen R. Lane. New York: Viking Pr., 1974. 148 p.

(original title: *Conjunciones y disyunciones*, 1969)

Essays on poetry, art, philosophy, the meaning of words, and other topics.

405. _____. *The labyrinth of solitude: Life and thought in Mexico.* Tr. Lysander Kemp. New York: Grove Pr., 1961. 212 p.

(original title: *El laberinto de la soledad*, 1950)

An established classic inquiry into the nature of the Mexican sense of identity. Highly poetic prose.

406. _____. *The other Mexico: Critique of the pyramid.* Tr. Lysander Kemp. New York: Grove Pr., 1972. 148 p.

(original title: *Posdata*, 1970)

Three essays and a postscript which complement *El laberinto de la soledad.* Develops ideas concerning the role of "third world" nations in determining man's future.

407. Reyes, Alfonso. *Mexico in a nutshell, and other essays.* Tr. Charles Ramsdell. Foreword Arturo Torres-Rioseco. Berkeley: Univ. of California Pr., 1964. vi, 145 p.

408. _____. *The position of America, and other essays.* Ed. and tr. Harriet de Onís. Foreword Federico de Onís. New York: Knopf, 1950. xii, 172 p. (rpt. Freeport, N.Y.: Books for Libraries, 1971)

Ten essays, including "Vision of Anahuac" ("Visión de Anáhuac," 1917). Highly lyrical prose. This volume includes a "Glossary of Proper Names" (pp. 165-172) which is useful.

409. Torri, Julio. *Julio Torri: Essays and poems.* Tr. and pref. Dorothy Margaret Kress. New York: Institute of French Studies, 1938. xi, 35 p.*

(original title: *Ensayos y poemas*, 1917)

Contains 22 prose poems or short essays.

410. Vasconcelos, José. *A Mexican Ulysses; an autobiography.* Tr. and abridged W. Rex Crawford. Bloomington, Indiana: Indiana Univ. Pr., 1963. 288 p. (rpt. New York: Greenwood Pr., 1972)

(original title: *Ulises criollo*, 1935)

Abridged version of Vasconcelos' autobiographical work. Reveals the development of ideas as well as interesting details of his life.

Nicaragua

411. Cardenal, Ernesto. *In Cuba.* Tr. and pref. Donald D. Walsh. New York: New Directions, 1974. 352 p.

(original title: *En Cuba*, 1973)

The account of the poet's visit to Cuba in 1970. Thoughts about life in a revolutionary society. Includes a glossary and a chronology of recent Cuban history.

412. Cardenal, Ernesto. *To live is to love*. Tr. Kurt Reinhardt. Intro. Thomas Merton. New York: Herder and Herder, 1972. 156 p. (rpt. New York: Image Books, 1974. 189 p. paper)

(original title: *Vida en el amor*, 1970)

Prose meditations. (Since January, 1973, original Herder and Herder volumes are published and distributed by Seabury Pr., New York.)

Uruguay

413. Rodó, José Enrique. *Ariel*. Tr. and intro. F. J. Stimson [J.S. of Dale]. Boston: Houghton-Mifflin, 1922. xxii, 150 p.*

(original title: *Ariel*, 1900)

Classic essay of the modernist period calling for the cultivation and development of conscience and spirit as opposed to materialism.

414. _____. *The motives of Proteus*. Tr. Angel Flores. Intro. Havelock Ellis. New York: Brentano's, 1928. xxvi, 378 p.

(original title: *Los motivos de Proteo*, 1909)

His major work in which he discusses the nature of conscience and spirit, and develops the concept of the "ethics of becoming" (ética del devenir).

II Brazilian Literature

A. Anthologies*

1. Mixed Genre

415. Cohen, J[ohn] M[ichael], ed. and intro. *Latin American writing today*. Harmondsworth & Baltimore: Penguin, 1967. 267 p. bibliog. paper (rpt. Gloucester, Mass.: Peter Smith, 1967, cloth)

Includes poetry selections by Carlos Drummond de Andrade and Vinicius de Moraes, a poetic play fragment by Joâo Cabral de Melo Neto, and prose selections by Joâo Guimarães Rosa, C. Vasconcelos Maia, and Breno Accioly.

416. *The literature of Latin America*. Washington, D.C.: Pan American Union, 1942. iii, 64 p.*

Includes a prose selection by Olavo Bilac, and poems by Augusto Frederico Schmidt and Augusto dos Anjos.

417. [*TriQuarterly*]. *The TriQuarterly anthology of contemporary Latin American literature*. Ed. José Donoso and William A. Henkin, with the staff of *TriQuarterly*. New York: E. P. Dutton, 1969,xi, 496 p. illus.

An outstanding collection of prose and poetry, including prose selections by Clarice Lispector, Nélida Piñón, Joâo Guimarães Rosa, and Dalton Trevisan.

2. Prose

418. Arciniegas, Germán, ed. *The green continent: A comprehensive view of Latin America by its leading writers*. Tr. Harriet de Onís *et al.* New York: Knopf, 1944. xiii, 533 p.* (rpt. London: Editions Poetry, 1947. 483 p.)

Prose selections by Euclydes da Cunha, José Pereira de Graça Aranha, Heitor Lyra, and Erico Verríssimo.
Essays and prose fiction of the first half of the twentieth century.

419. Flores, Angel and Dudley Poore, eds. *Fiesta in November; stories from Latin America*. Intro. Katherine Anne Porter. Boston: Houghton Mifflin, 1942. 608 p.*

A collection of stories and short novels which includes Jorge Amado's *Sea of the dead: Yemanja, mistress of the seas and the sails (Mar morto)*, tr. Donald Walsh.

*See the "Anthologies" section of "Spanish American Literature" for information regarding other writers. Isolated Brazilian contributions may be located by using the index of countries.

Jorge Amado is one of the most celebrated fiction writers of contemporary Brazil, and is widely translated.

420. Goldberg, Isaac, ed., tr. and intro. *Brazilian tales.* Boston: Four Seas, 1921. 149 p. (rpt. London: Allen and Unwin, 1924; rpt. Boston: International Pocket Library, 1965. 96 p. paper)

Includes 3 short stories by the master nineteenth-century Brazilian fiction writer Joaquim Maria Machado de Assis, and one each by José de Medeiros e Albuquerque, Coelho Netto, and Carmen Dolores.

421. Grossman, William L., ed., tr. and intro. *Modern Brazilian short stories.* Berkeley: Univ. of California Pr., 1968. © 1967 (London: Cambridge Univ. Pr., 1967)

Well chosen and translated collection of outstanding writers of early to recent periods of the twentieth century.

Collection of one story each by 17 writers. Bio-bibliographical sketches are included as endnotes. The authors are: Mário de Andrade, Darcy Azambuja, José Carlos Cavalcanti Borges, Ribeiro Couto, Aurélio Buarque de Holanda, Luís Jardim, Clarice Lispector, Aníbal Machado, Antônio de Alcântara Machado, R. Magalhães Júnior, Carlos Vasconcelos Maia, Marília São Paulo Penna e Costa, Rachel de Queiroz, Dinah Silveira de Queiroz, Graciliano Ramos, Marques Rebêlo, João Guimarães Rosa.

422. Howes, Barbara, ed. *The eye of the heart; short stories from Latin America.* Indianapolis-New York:

Bobbs-Merrill, 1973. xiv, 415 p. (rpt. New York: Avon, 1974)

Part of a fine anthology, a possible text for a literature in translation course at the university level.

Includes stories by Joaquim Maria Machado de Assis, Aníbal Monteiro Machado, João Guimarães Rosa, Dinah Silveira de Queiroz, Jorge Amado, Clarice Lispector.

423. Mancini, Pat McNees, ed. and intro. *Contemporary Latin American short stories.* Greenwich, Connecticut: Fawcett, 1974. 479 p. bibliog. paper

An excellent anthology of twentieth-century works. Includes selections by Joaquim Maria Machado de Assis, Jorge Amado, Clarice Lispector, and João Guimarães Rosa.

424. Onís, Harriet de, ed. and tr. *The golden land; an anthology of Latin American folklore in literature.* New York: Knopf, 1948. xviii, 395 p. (rpt. 1971)

Limited to early twentieth-century writers.

Includes prose selections by 6 Brazilian authors. They include: Euclydes da Cunha, Affonso Arinhos de Melo Franco, Gustavo Barroso, José Bento Monteiro Lobato, José Lins do Rego, and Mário de Andrade.

425. [Pinto], José Saldanha [da Gama] Coelho, comp. *Contistas brasileiros. New Brazilian short stories.* Tr. Rod W. Horton. Rio de Janeiro: Revista Branca, 1957. 238 p. illus.

The quality of selections by these modern writers is somewhat uneven.

Includes stories by Breno Accioly, José Maria Moreira Campo, Manuel Eduardo Pinheiro Campo, José Condé, Oswaldo Almeida Fischer, Carlos Vasconcelos Maia, José Saldanha da Gama Coelho Pinto, Murilo Rubião, Joel Ribeiro Silveira, Lygia Fagundes Teles.

3. Poetry

426. Bishop, Elizabeth and Emanuel Brasil, ed. and intro. *An anthology of twentieth-century Brazilian poetry.* Middletown, Connecticut: Wesleyan Univ. Pr., 1972. xxi, 181 p. bibliog.

A bilingual selection of 14 poets. English poems by 16 translators, many of them poets in their own right. The edition is complete with informative intro. and notes, complemented by a bibliography of works by the poets of the collection (pp. 175-177).

The poets are: Manuel Bandeira, Oswald de Andrade, Jorge de Lima, Mário de Andrade, Cassiano Ricardo, Joaquim Cardozo, Cecília Meireles, Murilo Mendes, Carlos Drummond de Andrade, Vinicius de Moraes, Mauro Mota, João Cabral de Melo Neto, Marcos Konder Reis, Ferreira Gullar.

427. Caracciolo-Trejo, Enrique, ed. *The Penguin book of Latin American verse.* Intro. Henry Gifford. Harmondsworth & Baltimore: Penguin, 1971. xlv, 424 p. index. paper

Selections cover Brazilian poetry from romanticism to contemporary expression.

Plain prose translations of the original texts.

Brazil is represented in this excellent anthology by the following poets: Antônio Gonçalves Dias, Olavo Bilac, Alphonsus de Guimaraens, Manuel Bandeira, Mário de Andrade, Cassiano Ricardo, Jorge de Lima, Cecília Meireles, Carlos Drummond de Andrade, Murilo Mendes, Augusto Frederico Schmidt, Vinicius de Moraes, João Carlos de Melo Neto.

428. Downes, Leonard Stephen, tr. *An introduction to modern Brazilian poetry; verse translations.* São Paulo: Clube de Poesia do Brasil (Poetry Club of Brazil), 1954. 86 p. illus.

Provides a panoramic view of trends in the poetry of the first half of the twentieth century.

No more than 2 selections by 50 poets. They are João Accioli, Guilherme Almeida, Carlos Drummond de Andrade, Mário de Andrade, Oswald de Andrade, Antônio Rangel Bandeira, Manuel Bandeira, Raul Bopp, Edgard Braga, Mário da Silva Brito, Geir Campos, Paulo Mendes Campos, Joaquim Cardozo, André Carneiro, Ronald de Carvalho, Darcy Damasceno, José Escobar Faria, José Paulo Moreira da Fonseca, Rossini Camargo Guarnieri, Alphonsus de Guimaraens Filho, Jamil Alman ir Haddad, Lêdo Ivo, Jorge de Lima, Henriqueta Lisboa, Fernando Ferreira de Loanda, Antônio Pinto de Medeiros, Cecília Meireles, João Cabral de Melo Neto, Murilo Mendes, Augusto Meyer, Dante Milano, Sérgio Milliet, José Tavares de Miranda, Vinicius de Moraes, Mauro Mota, Emilio Moura, Filipe d'Oliveira, Paulo Menotti del Picchia, Cyro Pimentel, Péricles Eugênio da Silva Ramos, Edson

Regis, Cassiano Ricardo, Bueno de Rivera, Augusto Frederico Schmidt, Domingo Carvalho da Silva, Tasso da Silveira, Alfonso Félix de Sousa, Milton de Lima Sousa, Geraldo Vidigal, Afrânio Zuccolotto.

429. Fitts, Dudley, ed. *Anthology of contemporary Latin American poetry. Antología de la poesía americana contemporánea.* Norfolk, Conn.: New Directions, 1942. 667 p.*

A bilingual edition which includes works by six modern Brazilian poets. They are: Carlos Drummond de Andrade, Manuel Bandeira, Ronald de Carvalho, Paulo Menotti del Picchia, Jorge de Lima, and Murilo Mendes.

430. Neistein, José, ed. *Poesia brasileira moderna: A bilingual anthology.* Tr. Manoel Cardozo. Washington, D.C.: Brazilian-American Cultural Institute, 1972. xii, 207 p.

Good selections from representative modern poets. Designed for the sophisticated and discerning reader. Includes introductions and bibliographical sketches of the poets.

Selections by: Mário de Andrade, Oswald de Andrade, Menotti Del Picchia, Guilherme de Almeida, Sérgio Milliet, Ronald de Carvalho, Manuel Bandeira, Cassiano Ricardo, Carlos Drummond de Andrade, Augusto Meyer, Jorge de Lima, Cecília Meireles, Vinicius de Moraes, João Cabral de Melo Neto, Péricles Eugênio de Silva Ramos, Máiro Faustino Lindolf Bell, Neide Archanjo, Mariajosé de Carvalho.

431. Nist, John and Yolanda Leite, ed. and tr. *Modern Brazilian poetry;*

an anthology. Intro John Nist. Bloomington, Indiana: Indiana Univ. Pr., 1962. 175 p. (rpt. Millwood, N.Y.: Kraus, 1968)

An excellent anthology which provides qualities of the survey with more depth than is usually offered.

Includes 110 selections by 12 poets. Biographical notes (pp. 169-175) are useful.

Poets are represented by 7 to 13 selections, except for João Cabral de Melo Neto, with only one extensive poem ("Only the blade of a knife," pp. 145-158). Other poets include: Manuel Bandeira, Mário de Andrade, Jorge de Lima, Cassiano Ricardo, Cecília Meireles, Carlos Drummond de Andrade, Murilo Mendes, Augusto Frederico Schmidt, Vinicius de Moraes, Domingos Carvalho da Silva, Paulo Bomfim.

432. Patterson, Helen Wohl, comp. and tr. *Poetisas de América.* Washington, D.C.: Mitchell Pr., 1960. 219 p. illus.*

A bilingual anthology of poetry by women which includes the work of two Brazilians: Cecília Meireles and Adalgisa Nery.

433. Poor, Agnes Blake, comp. *Pan American poems; an anthology.* Tr. Agnes Blake Poor and William Cullen Bryant. Boston: The Gorham Pr., 1918. 80 p.*

Brazilian poets included in the anthology are Antônio Gonçalves Dias and Francisco Manuel.

434. Trend, John Brande, comp. and tr. *Modern poetry from Brazil.* Cambridge: [Dolphin Book Co.], 1955. 32 p.

A bilingual edition, parallel texts. Poets include: Mário de Andrade, Manuel Bandeira, Ruy Ribeiro Couto, Jorge de Lima, Cecília Meireles, Augusto Frederico Schmidt.

Limited by the selection of only a few poems from the first half of the twentieth century.

435. *Young poetry of the Americas.* Vol. I. Washington, D.C.: Pan American Union, [196?], 116 p.*

A bilingual edition.

Includes the following short anthology of Brazilian verse: "Seven new Brazilian poets" (ed. Walmir Ayala), with poems by: Alberto da Costa e Silva, Fernando Mendez Viana, Lélia Coelho Frota, Mário Chimie, Mário Faustino, Marly de Oliveira, Octávio Mora.

Only a few selections by these lesser-known poets.

B. Individual Works

1. Novel

436. Alencar, José Martiniano de. *Iracema, the honeylips; a legend of Brazil.* Tr. Sir Richard and Isabel Burton. London: Bickers and Son, 1886. 106 p.

(original title: *Iracema; lenda do Ceará*, 1865)

A Romantic novel, a kind of prose poem of the arrival of Portuguese colonists in Brazil and the unification of races and cultures there.

437. _____. *Iracema; a legend of Ceará.* Tr. N. Bidell. Rio de Janeiro: Imprensa Inglesa, n.d. 114 p.

Trans. of *Iracema, lenda do Ceará.* See No. 436.

438. [Aguiar] Filho, Adonias. *Memories of Lazarus.* Tr. and intro. Fred P. Ellison. Austin: Univ. of Texas Pr., 1969. xiv, 170 p. illus.

(original title: *Memórias de Lázaro*, 1952)

A well-written novel of Bahia and the desolate and tragic life of that region. Nightmare imagery.

439. Almeida, Manuel Antônio de. *Memoirs of a militia sergeant.* Tr. Linton L. Barrett. Washington, D.C.: Pan American Union, 1959. xvi, 244 p.*

(original title: *Memórias de um sargento de milícias*, 1854)

Of the UNESCO Collection of Representative Works.

First published in serial form (newspapers) about Rio society during the first quarter of the nineteenth century.

440. Amado, Jorge. *Dona Flor and her two husbands; a moral and amorous tale.* Tr. Harriet de Onís. New York: Knopf, 1969. 553 p. glossary (London: Weidenfeld and Nicolson, 1969; rpt. New York: Bantam Books, 1971. paper)

(original title: *Dona Flor e seus dois maridos*, 1966)

Of contrasting life styles of the middle class in Salvador. An indirect protest of conditions in Bahia. Of considerable literary merit, and representative of more recent Amado novels in which the author avoids obvious accusation and denunciation of social evils.

Amado is one of Brazil's principal writers. His works have been translated into almost every major language.

441. Amado, Jorge. *Gabriela, clove and cinnamon*. Tr. William L. Grossman and James L. Taylor. New York: Knopf, 1962. viii, 425 p. (rpt. London: Chatto and Windus. 1963; rpt. Greenwich, England: Fawcett, 1969. 400 p. paper; rpt; New York: Avon, 1974, paper)

(original title: *Gabriela, cravo e canela*, 1958)
Of the effects of the modern age in Ilhéus during the first quarter of the twentieth century. A slightly picaresque tale of life in Bahia. Displays Amado's talent as a story teller and humorist.

442. _____. *Home is the sailor; the whole truth concerning the redoubtful adventures of Captain Vasco Moscoso de Aragão, master mariner.* Tr. Harriet de Onís. New York: Knopf, 1964. xv, 298 p. (London: Chatto and Windus, 1964)

2nd part of *Os velhos marinheiros* (1961): "A completa verdade sôbre as discutidas aventuras do Comandante Vasco Moscoso de Aragão, capitão de longo curso."
Amado creates a delightful hero, free in spirit and sensual. The first part of *Os velhos marinheiros* has also been translated into English. See No. 441.

443. _____. *Shepherds of the night*. Tr. Harriet de Onís. New York: Knopf, 1967, © 1966. xii, 364 p. glossary

(original title: *Os pastores da noite*, 1964)
A three-part novel providing a penetrating view of life in Bahia.

444. _____. *Tent of miracles*. Tr. Barbara Shelby. New York: Knopf, 1971. 380 p. glossary

(original title: *Tenda dos milagres*, 1969)
More complex in the use of time, place, and action, the novel relates the struggle of the people of Bahia to free themselves of poverty and misery.

445. _____ *The two deaths of Quincas Wateryell*. Tr. Barbara Shelby. New York: Knopf, 1965. 97 p. illus.*

(original title: "A Morte e a morte de Quincas Berro D'Agua," the 1st pt. of *Os velhos marinheiros: Duas histórias do cais de Bahia*, 1961)
An outstanding novella which provides insight into the quality of life.

446. _____. *The violent land*. Tr. Samuel Putnam. New York: Knopf, 1945. 335 p. glossary (rpt. with new foreword by author, 1965)

(original title: *Terras do sem fim*, 1943)
Of the conquest of cacau lands near Bahia at the beginning of the century. A critique of the feudal system of land ownership.

447. Andrade, Mário de. *Fräulein*. Tr. and adapted Margaret Richardson Hollingsworth. New York: Macaulay, 1933. 252 p.*

(original title: *Amar, verbo intransitivo*, 1927)
A somewhat satirical novel of manners of São Paulo. Fräulein is hired by the head of a family to educate his son to the dangers of women of the street.

448. Aranha, José Pereira da Graça. *Canaan*. Tr. Mariano Joaquín Lorente. Pref. Guglielmo Ferrera. Boston: Four Seas, 1920. 321 p.* (rpt. London: Allen and Unwin, 1921)

(original title: *Canaã*, 1902)
Of the disillusionment of German immigrants during the colonial period. Characterized by lyrical and philosophical elements.

449. Assis, Joaquim Maria Machado de. *Counselor Ayres' memorial*. Tr. and intro. Helen Caldwell. Berkeley: Univ. of California Pr., 1972. ix, 196 p.

(original title: *Memorial de Ayres*, 1908)
Machado de Assis' last novel, and one which is highly autobiographical in nature. More optimism than in other works.

450. _____. *Dom Casmurro*. Tr. Helen Caldwell. Intro. Waldo Frank. New York: Noonday Pr., 1953. 283 p. (Toronto: Longmans, 1953; London: W. H. Allen, 1953. 240 p.; rpt. New York: Noonday Pr., 1960. paper; rpt. Berkeley: Univ. of California Pr., 1966. 269 p.)

(original title: *Dom Casmurro*, 1900)
One of the author's masterpieces. A brilliant examination of the protagonist and the times in which he lives.

451. _____. *Epitaph of a small winner*. Tr. and intro. William L. Grossman. New York: Farrar and Straus, 1952. 223 p. illus. (Toronto: Longmans, 1952; rpt. London: W. H. Allen, 1953. 237 p.; rpt. New York: Noonday Pr., 1956. 223 p.

paper; rpt. Harmondsworth, England: Penguin, 1968. 235 p.)

(original title: *Memórias póstumas de Brás Cubas,* 1881)
A brilliant novel of a man's journey through a meaningless (both in personal and social terms) life.

452. _____. *Esau and Jacob*. Tr. and intro. Helen Caldwell. Berkeley: Univ. of California Pr., 1965. xx, 287 p. (rpt. London: Owen, 1966)

(original title: *Esaú e Jacó*, 1904)
Of twin brothers and their contrasting personalities. They are always in opposite camps. Strong element of humor.

453. _____. *The hand and the glove*. Tr. Albert I. Bagby, Jr. Foreword Helen Caldwell. Lexington, Kentucky: Univ. Pr. of Kentucky, 1970. xxii, 117 p.*

(original title: *A mão e a luva*, 1874)
Important for its role as one of Machado de Assis' first novels in the development of his style and themes.

454. _____. *Philosopher or dog? (Quinca Borba)*. Tr. Clotilde Wilson. New York: Farrar, Straus and Giroux, 1954. 271 p.* (As *The heritage of Quincas Borba*. London: W. H. Allen, 1954. 255 p.)

(original title: *Quincas Borba*, 1891)
Involves more action and offers less sarcasm than *Memórias póstumas de Brás Cubas*. A psychological study of Quincas Borba, who goes to Rio only to lose wealth, love, and sanity.

455. Assis, Joaquim Maria Machado de. *Posthumous reminiscences of Braz Cubas.* Tr. E. Percy Ellis. Rio de Janeiro: Ministério da Educação e Cultura, Instituto Nacional do Livro, 1955. 304 p.

(original title: *Memórias póstumas de Brás Cubas,* 1881)
See No. 451.

456. Azevedo, Aluízio de. *A Brazilian tenement.* Tr. Harry W. Brown. New York: Robert M. McBride, 1926. viii, 320 p.* (rpt. London: Cassell, 1928)

(original title: *O Cortiço,* 1890)
A Naturalist novel of life in Rio. Sordid details. Tragic lives.

457. Callado, Antônio Carlos. *Don Juan's Bar.* Tr. Barbara Shelby. New York: Knopf, 1972. 271 p.

(original title: *Bar Don Juan,* 1971)

Simultaneous narratives of Brazilian revolutionaries who plan to join Che Guevara in the Bolivian hinterland. Sympathetic, but not entirely idealistic, regarding the revolutionary cause in Latin America.

458. Callado, Antônio Carlos. *Quarup.* Tr. Barbara Shelby. New York: Knopf, 1970. 559 p.

(original title: *Quarup,* 1967)
Set in the Brazilian jungle, the novel relates the quest of various characters in developing personal and social values. Concludes with a very strong, political ending.

459. Carneiro, Cecílio. *The bonfire* (*A fogueira*). Tr. Dudley Poore. New York-Toronto: Farrar and Rinehart, 1944. 334 p. (rpt. London: Cassell, 1948. 297 p.; rpt. Westport, Conn.: Greenwood Pr., 1972. 334 p.)

(original title: *A fogueira,* 1941)
Received an honorable mention in the First Latin American Prize Novel Competition, 1941. Chronicles the life of a Syrian immigrant in Brazil.

460. Castro, Josué de. *Of men and crabs.* Tr. Susan Hertelendy. Pref. by author. New York: Vanguard Pr., 1970. xxiv, 190 p.

(original title: *Homens e caranguejos,* 1967)
By the noted social critic. A kind of novelistic study of life in the Northeast. Emphasizes social problems.

461. Corção, Gustavo. *My neighbor as myself.* Tr. Clotilde Wilson. London: Longmans, Green, 1957.

(original title: *A descoberta do outro,* 1944)
Memories in first person which relate the narrator's desire for happiness and freedom from the monotony of the technological society.

462. _____. *Who if I cry out.* Tr. and pref. Clotilde Wilson. Austin: Univ. of Texas Pr., 1967. x, 217 p.

(original title: *Liçoes de abismo,* 1951)
Memories and problems (moral, social, metaphysical) of a man who knows he is going to die.

463. Cruls, Gastão Luís. *The mysterious Amazonia; a Brazilian novel.* Tr. J. T. W. Sadler. Rio de Janeiro: Zélio Valverde, 1944. 263 p.

(original title: *A Amazônia misteriosa,* 1925)
A popular novel set in the jungle. Cruls has also published a study of

the flora, fauna, and Indian ethnography of the region.

464. Dourado, [Waldomiro] Autran. *A hidden life*. Tr. Edgar H. Miller, Jr. New York: Knopf, 1969. 150 p.

(original title: *Uma vida em segrêdo*, 1964)
Of the life of an orphaned country girl and her relatives who live in town. A sensitive and skillful study of characters and relationships at the turn of the century.

465. Freyre, Gilberto. *Mother and son; a Brazilian tale*. Tr. Barbara Shelby. New York: Knopf, 1967. 232 p.

(original title: *Dona Sinhá e o filho padre; seminovela*, 1964)
A first-person account which is a kind of mixture of historical novel (Recife at the end of the nineteenth century), sociological study, and essay. Freyre is recognized for his outstanding sociological studies of Brazil.

466. Gonzaga Filho, J. B. N. *The most charming woman; a novel for ladies*. Tr. Bella. Edinburgh and Glasgow: W. Hodge, 1913.

(original title unavilable)

467. Jesús, Carolina Maria de. *Child of the dark: The Diary of Carolina Maria de Jesús*. Tr. David St. Clair. New York: E. P. Dutton, 1962. 190 p. (rpt. New York: New American Library, 1969. 159 p.)

(original title: *Quarto de despejo: Diário de uma favelada,* 1960)
The graphic diary of slum life in São Paulo, narrated by the uneducated, unemployed mother of three illegitimate children.

468. Lispector, Clarice. *The apple in the dark*. Tr. and intro. Gregory Rabassa. New York: Knopf, 1967. (xvi), 361 p.*

(original title: *A maça no escuro*, 1961)
Of a murderer who seeks refuge. A novel of character analysis in an atmosphere of fear.

469. Marins, Francisco. *The mystery of the gold mines*. Tr. Eunice Siegel. London: Univ. of London Pr., 1962. 143 p. illus.

(original title unavailable)

470. Olinto, Antônio. *The water house*. Tr. Dorothy Heapy. London: Rex Collings, 1970. 410 p.

(original title: *A casa da agua*, 1969)
Novel of ex-slaves who return to their native Africa and must adapt themselves to their former homeland. Time span from 1898 to 1968.

471. Pereira, Antônio Olavo. *Marcoré*. Tr. Alfred Hower and John Saunders. Intro. Alfred Hower. Austin: Univ. of Texas Pr., 1970. xiv, 234 p. illus.

(original title: *Marcoré*, 1957)
Memoirs of family life in a small village of the interior. A perceptive and compassionate vision of the human condition.

472. Queiroz, Rachel de. *The three Marias*. Tr. Fred P. Ellison. Austin: Univ. of Texas Pr., 1963. xxiii, 178 p.

(original title: *As três Marias*, 1939)
An important novel of the "Northeast," in which three girls grow up and offer different views of reality.

473. Ramos, Graciliano. *Anguish*. Tr. L. C. Kaplan. New York: Knopf, 1946. 259 p. glossary. (rpt. Westport, Conn.: Greenwood Pr., 1972)

(original title: *Angústia*, 1936)
The novel had been published in English trans. two years earlier. Tr. Serafín J. García. Montevideo: Editorial Independencia, 1944. 248 p.
A psychological novel of frustration and murder.
A "glossary of Brazilian terms," is included (pp. 257-259).

474. _____. *Barren lives* (*Vidas sêcas*). Tr. and intro. Ralph Edward Dimmick. Austin: Univ. of Texas Pr., 1965. xxxiv, 131 p.

(original title: *Vidas sêcas*, 1938)
Excellent novel which reveals much about life in the Brazilian sertão. A national classic.

475. Rego [Cavalcanti], José Lins do. *Plantation boy*. Tr. Emmi Baum. New York: Knopf, 1966. 530 p. glossary*

Includes the author's "sugarcane cycle" of 3 novels: *Menino de engenho* (1932), *Doidinho* (1933), and *Bangüé* (1934). The novels offer a view of life on the plantation based on the author's life, from early childhood in the Northeast (*Menino de engenho*) including memories of school life (*Doidinho*) to a view of the decline of the feudal land system with the advent of industrialism.

476. _____. *Pureza*. Tr. Lucie Marion. London: Hutchinson International Authors, 1948. 176 p.

(original title: *Pureza*, 1937)

Psychological study of moral and spiritual disintegration.

477. Resende, Otto Lara. *The inspector of orphans*. Tr. Anne Cravinho. London: Deutsch, 1968. 254 p.

(original title: *O braço direito*, 1963)
Novel written in diary form which examines the problem of orphan children from the point of view of the administrator of the orphanage, and offers insight into life in a small provincial town. Awarded the Lima Barreto Prize in 1964.

478. Rosa, João Guimarães. *The Devil to pay in the backlands: The Devil in the street, in the middle of the whirlwind*. Tr. James A. Taylor and Harriet de Onís. New York: Knopf, 1963. 494 p.

(original title: *Grande sertão: Veredas*, 1956)
Widely acclaimed novel of life in rural Brazil. Exceptional for the author's use of language, probably the most innovative and influential in modern times. The translation of popular speech is an impossible task, otherwise the work is ably rendered into English.

479. Sabino, Fernando [Tavares]. *A time to meet*. Tr. John Proctor. London: Souvenir Pr., 1967. 319 p. (rpt. London: Panther, 1968. 268 p.)

(original title: *O encontro marcado*, 1956)
A psychological novel of characters who lack a sense of meaning in their lives.

480. Setúbal, Paulo de Oliveira.

Domitila; the romance of an Emperor's mistress. Tr., adapted, and prol. Margaret Richardson. New York: Coward-McCann, 1930. xi, 324 p.*

(original title: *A marqueza de Santos*, 1924)

A historical novel based on the life of Dom Pedro I, 1822-1829.

An appendix (pp. 304-324) includes explanatory notes about historical aspects of the novel.

481. Taunay, Alfredo d'Escragnolle [pseud. Sílvio Dinarte]. *Innocencia; a story of the prairie regions of Brazil.* Tr. James W. Wells. London: Chapman and Hall, 1889. 312 p.

(original title: *Inocéncia,* 1872)

Idealistic novel which may be seen as a novel of transition between Romanticism and Realism.

482. _____. *Inocéncia.* Tr. and pref. Henriqueta Chamberlain. New York: Macmillan, 1945. x, 209 p.*

(original title: *Inocência*, 1872; see No. 481)

483. Vasconcelos, José Mauro de. *My sweet-orange tree.* Tr. Edgar H. Miller, Jr. New York: Knopf, 1970. x, 213 p. illus.* (rpt. London: Joseph, 1971)

(original title: *Meu pé de laranja lima*, 1968)

A series of childhood memories of life in Rio. A prize-winning book of tenderness and love.

484. Veiga, José J. *The three trials of Manirema.* Tr. Pamela G. Bird. New York: Knopf, 1970. x, 154 p.

(original title: *A hora dos rumiantes*, 1966)

A town is mysteriously beset by three plagues in this allegorical novel.

485. Veríssimo, Erico. *Consider the lillies of the field.* Tr. Jean Neel Karnoff. New York: Macmillan, 1947. 371 p. (rpt. New York: Greenwood Pr., 1969)

(original title: *Olhai os lírios do campo*, 1938)

One of his most popular novels, though not his best. Embodies an idealistic vision of mankind.

Veríssimo is one of the most popular Brazilian novelists of the twentieth century.

486. _____. *Crossroads.* Tr. L. C. Kaplan. New York: Macmillan, 1943. 373 p. (rpt. as *Crossroads and destinies.* London: Arco, 1956; rpt. New York: Greenwood Pr., 1969)

(original title: *Caminhos cruzados*, 1935)

Reveals influence of cinematographic techniques. Good development of characters and situations.

487. _____. *His excellency, the ambassador.* Tr. Linton Lomas Barrett and Marie McDavid Barrett. New York-London: Macmillan, 1967. 439 p.*

(original title: *O senhor embaixador*, 1965)

The ambassador is of the imaginary Caribbean republic of Sacramento, ruled by a Castro-like revolutionary regime.

488. _____. *Night.* Tr. Linton Lomas Barrett. New York: Macmillan, 1956. 166 p* (rpt. London: Arco, 1956)

(original title: *Noite*, 1954)

An amnesia victim discovers the city at night.

489. Verrísimo, Erico. *The rest is silence*. Tr. L. C. Kaplan. New York: Macmillan, 1946. viii, 485 p. (rpt. London: Arco, 1956; rpt. New York: Greenwood, 1969)

(original title: *O resto é silêncio*, 1943)

Describes the city of Porto Alegre. Good portrayal of characters.

490. _____. *Time and the wind*. Tr. Linton Lomas Barrett. New York: Macmillan, 1951. 624 p. (rpt. London: Arco, 1954; rpt. New York: Greenwood Pr., 1969)

(original title: *O tempo e o vento*, 1949)

Chronicles the life of a gaucho family in a town on the southern frontier. Good characterizations.

2. Short Stories

491. Assis, Joaquim Maria Machado de. *The psychiatrist and other stories*. Tr. Helen Caldwell and William L. Grossman. Intro. William L. Grossman. Berkeley: Univ. of California Pr., 1963. x, 147 p. (rpt. London: Peter Owen, 1963)

Contains 12 selections from *Papéis avulsos* (1882) and other works. Proves the author to be an excellent writer of short fiction as well as novels.

492. _____. *What went wrong at the baroness'; a tale with a point*. Tr. Helen Caldwell. Santa Monica, California: Magpie Pr., 1963. 1 vol. unpaged. illus.*

493. Barroso, Gustavo. *Mapirunga*. Tr. R. B. Cunninghame Graham. London: Heinemann, 1942. 40 p.

(original title: *Mapirunga*)

Of tragedy in Brazil's frontier.

494. Duarte, Margarida Estrela Bandeira. *Legend of the palm tree*. Anon. trans. New York: Grosset and Dunlap, 1940. 47 p.*

(original title: *Lenda da carnaubeira*)

495. Jardim, Luís. *The armadillo and the monkey*. Tr. Maria Cimino. New York: Coward-McCann, 1942. 46 p.*

(original title: *O tato e o macaco*, 1940)

Retelling of a folktale; of special interest to children.

496. Lispector, Clarice. *Family ties*. Tr. and intro. Giovanni Pontiero. Austin: Univ. of Texas Pr., 1972. 156 p.

Trans. of the 13 stories of *Laços de família* (1960), highly subjective psychological studies of unquestionable literary merit.

497. Lobato, José Bento Monteiro. *Brazilian short stories*. Anon. trans. Intro. Isaac Goldberg. Girard, Kansas: Haldeman-Julius, 1925. 64 p.*

Contains 3 stories from *Urupês* (1918)

498. Reid, Lawrie. *My Lady Happiness, and other short stories*. Anon. trans. London: Batchworth, 1955. 225 p.

(original title: *Madona felicidade*, 1949)

A collection of 11 stories, including the title story.

499. Rosa, João Guimarães. *Sagarana*. Tr. Harriet de Onís. Intro. Franklin de Oliveira. New York: Knopf, 1966. xvi, 303 p.*

(original title: *Sagarana*, 1946; definitive ed., 1958)

Nine stories which establish Guimarães Rosa as one of the outstanding prose fiction writers in Brazil.

500. _____. *The third bank of the river, and other stories*. Tr. and intro. Barbara Shelby. New York: Knopf, 1968. xiv, 238 p.

(original title: *Primeiras estórias*, 1962)

Contains 22 stories. Guimarães Rosa's baroque style and popular speech are difficult to render into English.

501. Trevisan, Dalton. *The vampire of Curitiba and other stories*. Tr. Gregory Rabassa. New York: Knopf, 1972. 267 p.

Includes 44 stories from the revised and enlarged second editions (1970) of the following collections: *Novelas nada exemplares* (1959), *Cemitério de elefantes* (1964) [2nd ed. includes *Morte na Praça* (1964)], *O Vampiro de Curitiba* (1965), [2nd ed. includes *Desastres do amor* (1968)], and *A guerra conjugal* (1969).

The author, considered by many to be Brazil's leading contemporary short story writer, made slight manuscript changes especially for the English language editon.

502. Veiga, José J. *The misplaced machine and other stories*. Tr. Pamela G. Bird. New York: Knopf, 1970. viii, 141 p.

(original title: *A Máquina extraviada*, 1968)

Includes 14 stories. As in *The three trials of Manirema* (see No. 480) Veiga creates a sense of horror as characters become victims of evil forces.

3. Poetry

503. Andrade, Carlos Drummond de. *In the middle of the road: Selected poems of Carlos Drummond de Andrade*. Ed., tr. and intro. John Nist. Tucson, Arizona: Univ. of Arizona Pr., 1965. 121 p.

A bilingual edition of 63 poems by one of the most celebrated and controversial of Brazilian poets and a leader of the Modernist movement in Minas Gerais.

504. Andrade, Mário de. *Hallucinated city*. Tr. and intro. Jack E. Tomlins. Nashville, Tennessee: Vanderbilt Univ. Pr., 1968. 100 p.

(original title: *Paulicéia desvairada*, 1922)

A bilingual edition which includes the 22 poems and "Extremely interesting preface" which helped to launch Brazilian Modernism. Andrade's poems of São Paulo reflect his trend to develop a truly Brazilian literature in language, themes, and settings.

505. Leâo, Pedro Henrique Saraiva. *12 [Doze] poemas em inglês*. Anon.

trans. Fortaleza: Imprensa Universitária do Ceará, 1960. 55 p.

506. Lima, Jorge de. *Brazilian psalm.* Tr. Willis Wager. New York: G. Schirmer, 1941. 24 p.

Trans. of "Salmo," by Modernist Jorge de Lima.
His poetry developed into profoundly Christian thought expressed in characteristically Brazilian language.

507. _____. *Poems.* Tr. Melissa S. Hull. Rio de Janeiro, 1952. 56 p.

A selection of 23 poems, combining religious works with poems of local (regional) flavor.

508. Olinto, Antônio. *Theories and other poems.* Tr. Jean McQuillen. London: Rex Collings, 1972. 71 p.

A bilingual edition (parallel texts) with English verse translations.

4. Drama

509. Bloch, Pedro. *Enemies don't send flowers.* Tr. John Fostini. New York: The World's a Stage, 1957. typescript.*

(original title: *Os inimigos não mandam flores*, 1957)
Somewhat exaggerated psychological study of two characters.

510. _____. *The hands of Euridice; a play in two acts.* Tr. John Fostini. New York: The World's a Stage, 1957. typescript.*

(original title: *As mãos de Eurídice,* 1957)

Very well-received play with only one character. Another psychological study.

511. Callado, Antônio Carlos. *Frankel; a play in 3 acts.* Anon trans. Rio de Janeiro: Ministério da Educaçâo e Cultura, Serviço de Documentação, 1955. 89 p.

(original title: *Frankel*, 1955)
Examines the various problems concerning the question of limits of scientific experimentation on human subjects.

512. Figueiredo, Guilherme. *The fox and the grapes.* Tr. Jorge Cardoso Aires and John Fostini. New York: The World's a Stage, 1957. 106 p.*

(original title: *A raposa e as uvas*, 1953)
Shows more interest in ideas than dramatic effect.

513. _____. *A god slept here.* Tr. John Fostini. New York: The World's a Stage, 1957. typescript.*

(original title: *Um deus dormiu lá em casa*, 1957)
Figueiredo's version of the Amphitryon legend.

514. _____. *A god slept here.* Tr. Lloyd F. George. Rio de Janeiro: Ministério da Educação e Cultura, Serviço de Documentação, 1957. 106 p. illus.

(original title: *Um deus dormiu lá em casa*, 1957: see No. 513)

515. Gomes, Alfredo Dias. *Journey to Bahia.* Tr. and adapted Stanley

Richards. Washington, D. C.: Brazilian-American Cultural Institute, 1964. 79 p. illus.*

(original title: *O pagador de promessas*, 1960)
Virtue is not rewarded in this play which highlights social injustice in a peasant's dealings with Church officials.

516. Miranda, Edgard da Rocha. *. . . and the wind blew; a play in three acts*. Anon trans. Rio de Janeiro: Ministério da Educação e Cultura, Serviço de Documentação, 1958. 158 p. illus.

(original title unavailable)

517. Paula, José Agrippino de. *The United Nations*. Tr. John Proctor. Rio de Janeiro: Tridente, 1967.

(original title: *Pan América*, 1967)

518. Suassuna, Ariano. *The rogue's trial: The crimes of John Crickett and other rogues; Their trial and the intercession of Mary, our Lady of Mercy. A satire on human frailties in the form of a miracle play based on the ballads and folk tales of Northeastern Brazil*. Tr. and intro. Dillwyn F. Ratcliff. Berkeley: Univ. of California Pr., 1963. 107 p.

(original title: *Auto da compadecida*, 1957)
Author combines techniques of the puppet show, the miracle play, and *commedia dell'arte* with Brazilian folklore. Based on a fifteenth-century *auto* by Gil Vicente, but Brazilian in feeling and social satire.

5. Essay*

519. Castro, Josué de. *The black book of hunger*. Tr. Charles Lam Markmann. New York: Funk and Wagnalls, 1968, © 1967. xiii, 161 p.

(original title: *O livro negro de fome*, 1960)
His novel *Of men and crabs* (see No. 456) is based on the writer's keen awareness of socio-economic problems in Brazil.

520. Cunha, Euclydes da. *Rebellion in the backlands*. Tr. and intro. Samuel Putnam. Chicago: Univ. of Chicago Pr., 1944. xxiii, 526 p.* (rpt. 1970. paper; abridged ed. London, 1947)

(original title: *Os sertões*, 1902)
An imposing account, enhanced by certain novelistic techniques, of 4 government expeditions sent to the sertão of northern Bahia to capture Antônio Maciel, leader of roving outlaws (jagunços). A very influential work in the history of Brazilian thought and literature.

521. Freyre, Gilberto. *The masters and the slaves: A study in the development of Brazilian civilization*. Tr. Samuel Putnam. New York: Knopf, 1946. xliv, 537 p. (London: Secker, 1947. [rpt. (from 2nd abridged ed. of original) New York: Knopf, 1964. 432 p.]

(original title: *Casa grande e senzala*, def. ed. 1943)
Monumental study of Brazilian civilization.

522. Moog, Clodomir Vianna. *Bandeirantes and pioneers*. Tr. L. L.

*A selected list.

523-524

Barret. New York: Braziller, 1964. 316 p.

(original title: *Bandeirantes e pioneiros*, 1954)
Comparison of North American and Brazilian cultures.

523. Neto, Bento Munhoz da Rocha. *An interpretation of the Americas.* Tr. Charles Fulton. Rio de Janeiro and New York: Euro-American, 1957. 183 p.*

524. Ramos, Graciliano. *Jail: Prison memoirs.* Tr. Thomas Colchie. New York: Evans, 1974.

(original title: *Memórias do cárcere*, 1953)
Listed in *1974 Books in Print* but unconfirmed.
Memórias do cárcere is an important essay collection of high literary quality.

III Non-Hispanic Literature of the Caribbean Islands and Guyanas

A. Anthologies*

1. Mixed Genre

525. Coulthard, G. R., ed. and tr. *Caribbean literature; an anthology*. London: Univ. of London Pr., 1966. 128 p.

A collection of prose, poetry and drama. Includes selections by Aimé Césaire (Martinique) and Jacques Roumain (Haiti).

526. Howes, Barbara, ed. *From the green Antilles*. New York: Macmillan, 1966. 368 p.*

Selections of prose and poetry. Many translators. Includes works by Aimé Césaire (Martinique), Gilbert de Chambertrand (Guadeloupe), Pierre Duprey (Martinique), Albert Helman (Surinam), Boeli van Leeuwen (Netherlands Antilles), Magloire-Saint-Aude (Haiti), Tip Marugg (Curaçao) [sic], Florette Morand (Guadeloupe), Clément Richer (Martinique), René de Rooy (Surinam-Curaçao), St.-John Perse (Guadeloupe), Raphaël Tardon (Martinique), Philippe Thoby-Marcelin (Haiti), Joseph Zobel (Martinique).

2. Poetry

527. Collins, Marie, ed. *Black poets in French*. New York: Scribner's, 1972. xviii, 165 p. photos

A bilingual edition of Caribbean and African poets. Those from the Caribbean are: Léon Damas (French Guiana), Aimé Césaire (Martinique), Jacques Roumain (Haiti), Jean Brierre (Haiti), René Depestre (Haiti), Anthony Phelps (Haiti), Paul Niger (Guadeloupe), Guy Tirolien (Guadeloupe).

Most of the selections are by Damas and Césaire.

528. Figueroa, John, comp. *Caribbean voices: Dreams and visions*. Vol. I. London: Evans Bros., 1966. 119 p. paper

*For anthologies which include selections by Spanish American authors, see the "Anthologies" section of Part I.

The first of two volumes of selected Caribbean poets, almost entirely of English-speaking writers. The anthology includes poems by Gilbert de Chambertrand (Guadeloupe) and Gilbert Gratiant (Martinique).

529. Fitts, Dudley, ed. *Anthology of contemporary Latin American poetry. Antología de la poesía americana contemporánea.* Norfolk, Conn.: New Directions, 1942. 667 p. (rev. ed., 1947, 677 p.)*

A bilingual editon. Includes selections by Haitian poets Jacques Roumain, Emile Roumer, and Duraciné Vaval.

530. Hughes, Langston and Arna Bontemps, eds. *The poetry of the negro, 1746-1949.* New York: Doubleday, 1949. 429 p.*

Various translators. Poems by: Jean Brierre (Haiti), Roussan Camille (Haiti), Aimé Césaire (Martinique), Léon Damas (French Guiana), Oswald Durand (Haiti), Luc Grimard (Haiti), Louis Morpeau (Haiti), Ignace Nau (Haiti), Charles F. Pressoir (Haiti), Jacques Roumain (Haiti), Emile Roumer (Haiti), Normil Sylvain (Haiti), Philippe Thoby-Marcelin (Haiti), Isaac Toussaint-L'Ouverture (Haiti), Duraciné Vaval (Haiti), Christian Werleigh (Haiti).

531. Jones, Edward Allen, ed. and tr. *Voices of négritude: The expression of black experience in the poetry of Senghor, Césaire, and Damas.* Valley Forge, Penn.: Judson Pr., 1971. 125 p. bibliog. paper

A literary study of the poetry of Aimé Césaire (Martinique), Léon Damas (French Guiana) and African poet Senghor. Included are several translations of their work. The book also contains selections by additional Caribbean poets. They include: Guy Tirolien (Guadeloupe), Paul Niger (Guadeloupe), Jean Brierre (Haiti), and Jacques Roumain (Haiti).

532. Murphy, Beatrice M., ed. *Ebony rhythm: An anthology of contemporary Negro verse.* New York: Exposition Pr., 1948. 161 p. (rpt. Freeport, N.Y.: Books for Libraries, 1968)

Includes selections by Jean Brierre (Haiti).

533. Patterson, Helen Wohl, comp. and tr. *Poetisas de América.* Washington, D.C.: Mitchell Pr., 1960. 219 p. illus.*

Bilingual edition. Includes poems by Haitian poets Marie-Thérèse Colimon, Emmeline Carriès Lemaire, and Virginie Sempeur.

534. Ruiz del Vizo, Hortensia, ed. *Black poetry of the Americas (a bilingual anthology).* Miami: Ediciones Universal, 1972. 176 p. paper

Trilingual edition (poems in original French are translated into Spanish and English). Includes selections by Léon Damas (French Guiana), Guy Tirolien (Guadeloupe), Gilbert de Chambertrand (Guadeloupe), Emmanuel-Flavia Léopold (Martinique), Etienne Lero (Martinique), Jacques Roumain (Haiti), Duraciné Vaval (Haiti), Emile Roumer (Haiti).

For reference to selections from black poets of Spanish America, see No. 63a.

535. Shapiro, Norman R., ed. and tr. *Négritude: Black poetry from Africa and the Caribbean.* Intro. Wilfred Cartey. New York: October House, 1970. 240 p.*

A bilingual anthology which also includes African poets. Caribbean poets are: Jean Brierre (Haiti), Carl Brouard (Haiti), Roussan Camille (Haiti), Aimé Césaire (Martinique), Henri Corbin (Guadeloupe), Léon Damas (French Guiana), René Depestre (Haiti), Auguste Desportes (Martinique), Jocelyn Etienne (Guadeloupe), Gilbert Gratiant (Martinique), Gabrielle Jos (Guadeloupe), Léon Laleau (Haiti), Frantz Leroy (Haiti), Rudolph Moïse (Haiti), Paul E. Najac (Haiti), Louis Neptune (Haiti), Anthony Phelps (Haiti), René Philoctète (Haiti), Joseph Polius (Martinique), Marie-Thérèse Rouil (Martinique), Guy Tirolien (Guadeloupe).

536. Underwood, Edna W., ed. and tr. *The poets of Haiti, 1782-1934.* Portland, Maine: The Mosher Pr., 1934. 159 p.*

Includes selections by the following poets: Macdonald Alexander, Fernand Ambroise, Louis Borno, Jean Brierre, Carl Brouard, Frédéric Burr-Reynaud, Adrian Carrénard, Maurice Casséus, Pascal Casséus, Roland Chassagne, Arsène Chevry, Massilon Coicou, Louis-Henri Durand, Oswald Durand, Luc Grimard, Tertullien Guilbaud, Dominique Hippolyte, Edmund La Forest, Léon Laleau, Robert Lataillade, George Lescouflair, Paul Lochard, Léon Louhis, Clément Magloire-Fils, Victor Mangonés, Constantin Mayard, Pierre Mayard, Charles Moravia, Louis Morpeau,

Ignace Nau, Edgard Numa, Timothée Paret, Charles F. Pressoir, Christian Regulies, Justinien Ricot, Volvick Ricourt, Milo Rigaud, Jacques Roumain, Emile Roumer, George Sylvain, Normil Sylvain, Philippe Thoby-Marcelin, Isaac Toussaint-L'Ouverture, Duraciné Vaval, Damoclès Vieux, Etzer Vilaire, Jean-Joseph Vilaire, Christian Werleigh.

537. Wolitz, Seth L., tr. *Black poetry of the French Antilles: Haiti, Martinique, Guadeloupe, Guiana.* Berkeley: Fybate Lecture Notes, 1967. 37 p.

Limited edition of 497 copies. Includes poems by René Bélance (Haiti), Jean Brierre (Haiti), Roussan Camille (Haiti), Aimé Césaire (Martinique), Léon Damas (French Guiana), Gilbert Gratiant (Martinique), Etienne Lero (Martinique), Jacques Roumain (Haiti), Guy Tirolien (Guadeloupe).

538. *Young poetry of the Americas.* Vol. I. Washington, D.C.: Pan American Union, (196?) 116 p.*

A bilingual edition which includes the following brief anthology: "Five Haitian poets" (ed. Maurice A. Lubin) with poems by Jean Richard Laforest, René Philoctète, Roland Morisseau, Anthony Phelps, and Jeanine Tavernier Louis.

B. Individual Works

1. Fiction

Haiti

539. Chauvet, Marie. *Dance on the*

volcano. Tr. Salvator Attanasio. New York: Sloane, 1959. 376 p.*

(original title: *La Danse sur le volcan*, 1957)

Young free octoroon girl singer active in white theatre as revolution begins. An historical novel based on persons and events in Haiti of the 1780's.

540. Roumain, Jacques. *Masters of the dew*. Tr. Langston Hughes and Mercer Cook. Intro. Mercer Cook. New York: Reynal & Hitchcock, 1947. x, 180 p. (rpt. New York: Collier Books, 1971. 192 p. paper)

(original title: *Gouverneurs de la rosée*, 1946)

Marxist novel. Hero who learned of class solidarity in Cuba and returns to Haiti and dies a martyr to scientific irrigation. Contemporary.

541. Thoby-Marcelin, Philippe and Pierre Marcelin. *All men are mad*. Tr. Eva Thoby-Marcelin. Intro. Edmund Wilson. New York: Farrar, Straus & Giroux, 1970. xii, 179 p. glossary

(original title: *Tous les hommes sont fous*)

French priest tries to eradicate spiritism in Haiti. Historical references to events of 1942.

542. _____. *The beast of the Haitian hills*. Tr. Peter C. Rhodes. New York: Rinehart and Co., 1946. 213 p.* (rpt. New York: Time, 1964. 172 p.)*

(original title: *La bête du musseau*, 1946)

City grocer goes to live among peasants and is destroyed by a peasant in league with evil spirits. Contemporary Haiti.

543. _____. *Canapé-vert*. Tr. Edward LaRocque Tinker. New York: Farrar & Rinehart, 1944. 225 p.*

(original title: *Canapé-vert*, 1944)

Voodoo and witchcraft among Haitian farmers. Contemporary.

544. _____. *Pencil of God*. Tr. Leonard Thomas. Boston: Houghton-Mifflin, 1951. 204 p.*

(original title: *Le Crayon de Dieu*)

African spells play havoc among city-dwellers in contemporary Haiti.

545. _____. *The singing turtle and other tales from Haiti*. Tr. Eva Thoby-Marcelin. New York: Farrar, Straus & Giroux, 1971. 115 p.

(original title: *Contes et légendes d'Haïti*, 1967)

Stories from Haitian folklore.

Martinique

546. Glissant, Edouard. *The ripening*. Tr. Frances Frenaye. New York: George Braziller, 1959. 253 p.*

(original title: *La Lézarde*, 1958)

Young people active in electoral politics; contemporary Martinique. Original title refers to the name of the river in whose vicinity the novel is set.

547. Maran, René. *Batouala*. Tr. Alvah C. Bessie. New York: Limited Editions Club, 1932. 117 p.*

(original title: *Batouala; véritable roman nègre*, 1921)

An account of life in a native

village in French Equatorial Africa. Strongly anticolonial.

548. Maran, René. *Batouala*. Tr. Adele Szold Seltzer. New York: T[homas] Seltzer, 1922, 207 p. (rpt. New York: A. & C. Boni, 1930; rpt. New York: Thomas Seltzer, 1952; rpt. Port Washington, New York: Kennikat Pr., 1969)*

See No. 547.

549. _____. *Batouala; a negro novel from the French of René Maran.* [Anon. trans.] London: Jonathan Cape, [1922]. 192 p.

See No. 547.

550. _____. *Batouala; a true black novel.* Tr. Barbara Beck and Alexandre Mboukou. Washington: Black Orpheus Pr., 1972. 149 p. (rpt. London: Heinemann Educational Books, 1973. 135 p.; rpt. Greenwich, Conn.: Fawcett, 1974)

A new translation of the *édition définitive* (Paris: Michel, 1938). See No. 547.

551. Richer, Clément. *Son of Ti-Coyo.* Tr. Gerard Hopkins. New York: Knopf, 1954. 245 p. (London: Hart, Davis, 1954)*

(original title: *Nouvelles aventures de Ti-Coyo et de son requin*)
A continuation of No. 552.

552. _____. *Ti-Coyo and his shark; an immoral fable.* Tr. Gerard Hopkins. New York: Knopf, 1951. 235 p.*

(original title: *Ti-Coyo et son requin*, 1941)
Small boy trains his pet shark to devour his competitors in diving for coins thrown by tourists from ocean liners in the bay of Port-de-France.

He eventually becomes rich and respectable.

553. Schwarz-Bart, Simone. *The bridge of beyond.* Tr. Barbara Bray. New York: Atheneum, 1974. 246 p.

(original title: *Pluie et vent sur Télumée Miracle*, 1972)
Part of a series with André Schwarz-Bart as co-author entitled "La mulâtesse solitude."

Netherlands Antilles

554. Marugg, Tip. *Weekend pilgrimage.* Tr. Roy Edwards. London: Hutchinson and Co., 1960. 191 p.

(original title: *Weekend pelgrimage; roman*, 1957 [serial], 1958)

2. Poetry

Cuba

555. Hérédia, José-María de. *The conquerors.* Tr. Edward Robeson Taylor. San Francisco: E. R. Taylor, 1896. (10 leaves)*

Selections from *Les trophées*, 1893.
Hérédia (1842-1905), Cuban-born leader of French Parnassian poetry, should not be confused with his cousin, José María Heredia (1803-1839), a precursor of Spanish American romanticism.

556. _____. *Translations from José-María de Hérédia.* Tr. Merle St. Croix Wright. New York: H. Vinal, 1927. 122 p. illus.*

A bilingual edition of selected poems. Only 450 copies.

557. _____.*Sonnets of José-María de Hérédia.* Ed., tr. and pref. Edward

Robeson Taylor. San Francisco: W. Doxey, 1897, xiii, 177p. (2nd ed., 1898. xiv, 182 p.; 3rd ed. as *Sonnets from 'The trophies' of José-María de Hérédia*. San Francisco: P. Elder & M. Shepard, 1902. 176 p.; 4th ed. San Francisco: P. Elder & Co., 1906; 5th ed. San Francisco: (by author), 1913, xxiii, 193 p.)*

(original title: *Les trophées*, 1893)
Each subsequent edition (except the 4th) is slightly revised. They contain all 118 sonnets from the original collection.

558. Hérédia, José-María de. *Les trophées. The sonnets*. Tr. Henry Johnson. New Haven, Conn.: Yale Univ. Pr., 1910. 156 p.*

A bilingual edition.

559. _____. *The trophies; fifty sonnets*. Tr. and intro. Brian Hill. Philadelphia: Dufour, 1962. 73 p. (London: Rupert Hart-Davis, 1962)

Bilingual selections from *Les trophées*, 1893.

560. _____. *The trophies; sonnets*. Tr. Frank Sewail. Boston: Small, Maynard, 1900. xv, 133 p.*

Selections from *Les trophées*, 1893. Limited edition of 750 copies.

561. _____. *The trophies, with other sonnets*. Tr. John Myers O'Hara and John Hervey. New York: John Day, 1929. lxii, 241 p. illus.*

Includes the poems of *Les trophées* (1893) and other works.

French Guiana

562. Damas, Léon [Gontran]. *African songs of love, war, grief, and abuse*. Tr. Ulli Beier and Miriam Koshland. Evanston, Illinois: Northwestern Univ. Pr., 1963. 40 p. paper*

Guadeloupe

563. Perse, Saint-John [pseud. of Alexis Saint-Léger Léger]. *Anabase*. [Anon. trans.] New York: Brentano's, 1945. 75p.*

(original title: *Anabase*, 1924)
Born in Guadeloupe, St.-John Perse lived most of his life in France, and served in the French diplomatic corps. He received the Nobel Prize for Literature in 1960, and has been widely translated throughout the world. His poetry stresses the universality of man and his most basic concerns.

564. _____. *Anabasis*. Tr. T. S. Eliot. London: Faber and Faber, 1930. (rev. ed. New York: Harcourt, 1938. 75 p.; rev. and corrected ed. New York: Harcourt, 1949. 109 p.)*

Bilingual edition of *Anabase*, 1924.

565. _____. *Birds*. Tr. Robert Fitzgerald. New York: Pantheon, 1966. 71 p. plates, bibliog.

Bilingual edition of *L'Ordre des oiseaux*, 1962.

566. _____. *Birds*. Tr. J. Roger Little. Durham: North Gate Pr., 1967. 19 p.*

Selections from *L'Ordre des oiseaux*, 1962.
Limited edition of 103 copies.

567. Perse, Saint-John [pseud. of Alexis Saint-Léger Léger]. *Chronique*. Tr. Robert Fitzgerald. New York: Pantheon, 1961. 60 p. bibliog.

Bilingual edition of *Chronique*, 1959.

568. _____. *Collected poems*. Tr. W. H. Auden *et al*. Princeton, N.J.: Princeton Univ. Pr., 1971. 682 p.

Includes all of the translations published separately in book form, with additional poems, essays, and prefaces to their translations by T. S. Eliot and Louise Varèse.
All the translations have been revised for the collected works, and approved by the poet himself.

569. _____. *Eloges and other poems*. Tr. Louise Varèse. New York: Norton, 1944. 179 p. (rev. ed. New York: Pantheon Pr., 1956. 103 p.; rev. ed. with intro. by Archibald MacLeish, 1965. 104 p.)

Bilingual edition of *Eloges*, 1911, 1925, rev. ed. 1948.

570. _____. *Exile and other poems*. Tr. Denis Devlin, New York: Pantheon, 1949. 166 p. (rpt. 1962. 99 p.)

Bilingual edition of *Exil*, 1942.
The first English edition is a deluxe edition for collectors.

571. _____. *Seamarks*. Tr. Wallace Fowlie. New York: Pantheon, 1958. 363 p.*

Bilingual edition of *Amers*, 1957.

572. _____. *Winds*. Tr. Hugh Chisholm. New York: Pantheon, 1953. 252 p. (rpt. 1961. 193 p.)*

Bilingual edition of *Vents*, 1946.

Haiti

573. Depestre, René. *A rainbow for the Christian west*. Tr. Jack Hirschman. Fairfax and Los Angeles: Red Hill Pr., 1972. 64 p. paper

(original title: *Un Arc-en-ciel pour l'occident chrétien*, 1967)
Depestre is known as one of the region's most talented young revolutionary poets.

574. Roumain, Jacques. *Ebony wood. Bois d'ébène. Poems by Jacques Roumain*. Tr. Sidney Shapiro. New York: Interworld Pr., 1972. 45 p.

A bilingual edition.

Martinique

575. Césaire, Aimé. *Cadastre; poems*. Tr. Emile Snyder and Sanford Upson. Intro. Emile Snyder. New York: Third Pr., 1973.

(original title: *Cadastre*, 1961; a reissue of *Soleil cou coupé* (1949) and *Corps perdu* (1949))
A bilingual collection of 53 poems from the two works. Occasional notes by the translators.

576. _____. *Cahier d'un retour au pays natal; précédé par 'Un grand poète noir,' par André Breton*. Tr. Lionel Abel and Ivan Goll [sic]. New York: Brentano's, 1947. unpaged

Bilingual edition. Title in English: *Memorandum on my Martinique*.

577. Césaire, Aimé. *Cahier d'un retour au pays natal. Return to my native land*. Tr. Emile Snyder. Pref. André Breton. Paris: Présence Africaine, 1971. 155 p.

(original title: *Cahier d'un retour au pays natal*, 1947)

The trans. is based on the 1947 translation (see No. 576), incorporating changes in the *édition définitive* (Paris: Présence Africaine, 1956). A bilingual edition.

Césaire's famous poem, first published in periodical form (1939), then as a book, is now considered a document which is prophetic of the *négritude* movement.

578. _____. *Return to my native land*. Tr. John Berger and Anna Bostock. Intro. Mazisi Kunene. Harmondsworth & Baltimore: Penguin, 1969. 95 p. paper

(original title: *Cahier d'un retour au pays natal*, 1947)

A new translation of No. 577.

579. _____. *State of the union*. Ed. and tr. Clayton Eshleman and Denis Kelly. Cleveland: Caterpillar, 1966.*

Poems selected from *Les Armes miraculeuses* (1947), *Cadastre* (1961), and *Ferrements* (1960).

580. Laviaux, Léon. *The ebon muse, and other poems*. Tr. John Myers O'Hara. Portland, Maine: Smith and Sale, 1914. 51 p.*

A limited edition of 200 copies.

3. Drama

Martinique

581. Césaire, Aimé. *A season in the Congo*. Tr. Ralph Manheim. New York: Grove Pr., 1969, © 1968, 104 p.

(original title: *Une saison au Congo*, 1967)

Based on the life of Patrice Lumumba.

582. _____. *The tragedy of King Christophe*. Tr. Ralph Manheim. New York: Grove Pr., 1970, © 1969. 96 p.

(original title: *La tragédie du roi Christophe*, 1953)

Of the struggle for independence in Haiti and the king's personal defects which lead to his downfall.

IV. Appendix

A. Indian Literature of Latin America in English Translation: A Selected Reading List

583. Berg, Stephen, tr. *Nothing in the word: Versions of Aztec poetry*. New York: Grossman, 1972. 1 vol. unpaged; collages (Tokyo: Mushinsha Ltd., 1972)

A beautifully illustrated edition of 50 short poems and songs. Translations based generally on Spanish translations by Angel María Garibay K. (*Poesía nahuatl*). A collector's item.

584. Bierhorst, John, ed., tr. and foreword. *Four masterworks of American Indian literature: Quetzalcoatl; The ritual of condolence; Cuceb; The night chant*. New York: Farrar, Straus, and Giroux, 1974. xxiv, 371 p. bibliogs.

Scholarly presentation, including new English translation, of each work, with separate introduction, notes, and bibliography. The masterworks are from Aztec, Iroquois, Maya, and Navajo cultures, respectively. *Cuceb* is a revision of the English translation by Ralph L. Roys (1949).

585. Bierhorst, John, ed. and intro. *In the trail of the wind: American Indian poems and ritual orations*. New York: Farrar, Straus and Giroux, 1971. xi, 201 p.

Well-annotated edition which includes 18 Aztec, 6 Maya, and other poems of Indian cultures from Latin America.

586. *The book of Chilam Balam of Chumayel*. Ed., tr. and intro. Ralph L. Roys. Additional intro. J. Eric S. Thompson. Norman: Univ. of Oklahoma Pr., 1967. xvi, 229 p. bibliog.

Scholarly edition in Maya and English of this important Mayan work.

587. *The book of counsel: The Popol Vuh of the Quiché Maya of Guatemala*. Ed., tr. and intro. Munro S. Edmonson. New Orleans: Middle American Research Institute, Tulane University, 1971. xvii, 273 p. bibliog.*

Informative introduction to the work that has inspired the novels and stories of Nobel Prize winner Miguel Angel Asturias (Guatemala). The *Popol Vuh* appeared in

English translation earlier. See: *Popol Vuh: The sacred book of the ancient Quiche Maya*. English version Delia Goetz and Sylvanus G. Morley from the trans. (into Spanish) of Adrián Recinos. Norman: Univ. of Oklahoma Pr., 1950. xix, 267 p.

588. Brandon, ed. and comp. *The magic world: American Indian songs and poems*. New York: William Morrow, 1971. xiv, 145 p.

Contains 9 Nahuatl selections, 3 Maya poems, and others.

589. Brinton, Daniel G., ed., tr. and intro. *Ancient Nahuatl poetry; containing the Nahuatl texts of XXVII ancient Mexican poems*. Philadelphia: Library of Aboriginal American Literature, 1887. Vol. VII. viii, 177 p. vocabulary (facs. rpt. New York: AMS Pr., 1969)

A bilingual text of 27 poems and songs. One of the earliest studies and English translations of Nahuatl poetry.

590. _____, ed., tr. and intro. *The Maya chronicles*. Philadelphia: D. G. Brinton, Library of Aboriginal American Literature, 1882. Vol. I. vii, 279 p. vocabulary

Includes 5 selections from 3 Maya texts, with commentary.

591. Gerez, Toni de, tr. *2-Rabbit, 7-wind: Poems from ancient Mexico, retold from Nahuatl texts*. New York: Viking Pr., 1971. 56 p.

Selected and revised fragments based on texts of Sahagún, Garibay and León-Portilla.

592. Goetz, Delia and Adrián

Recinos, tr. [from Cakchiquel-Maya]. *The annals of the Cakchiquels*; with *Totonicapán*, tr. from Quiché text into Spanish by Dionisio José Chonay. English version Delia Goetz. Norman: Univ. of Oklahoma Pr., 1953.

593. *The güegüence; a comedy ballet in the Nahuatl-Spanish dialect of Nicaragua*. Ed., tr. and intro. Daniel G. Brinton. Philadelphia: D. G. Brinton (Library of Aboriginal American Literature, 1883. Vol. III. lii, 94 p. (facs. rpt. New York: AMS Pr., 1969)*

Bilingual edition based on the 1874 text of *El baile del güegüence; o Macho-Ratón*.

594. León-Portilla, Miguel, ed. *The broken spears: The Aztec account of the conquest of Mexico*. Tr. [into Spanish] Angel María Garibay K. Tr. (into English) Lysander Kemp. Boston: Beacon Pr., 1962. xxxi, 168 p. illus. bibliog.

Trans. of the Mexican edition of *Visión de los vencidos*, 1959)

595. _____, ed. *Pre-Columbian literatures of Mexico*. Tr. Grace Lobanov and Miguel León-Portilla. Norman: Univ. of Oklahoma Pr., 1969. xiii, 191 p. bibliog.

A revised edition of León-Portilla's *Las literaturas precolombinas de México* (1964) intended for an English-speaking public. Includes myths, sacred hymns, lyric poetry, rituals, chronicles, and other forms of prose. Numerous selections.

596. Nicholson, Irene. *Firefly in the night: A study of ancient Mexican poetry and symbolism*. London:

Faber and Faber, 1959. 231 p. illus. bibliog.

An interesting study of the culture and poetry of the Aztecs with many translations of poem fragments. Well indexed with a selected bibliography.

597. Rothenberg, Jerome, comp. *Shaking the pumpkin: Traditioinal poetry of the Indian North Americas*. Garden City, N.Y.: Doubleday, 1972. xxvi, 475 p. illus.

Well-annotated edition. Includes 25 selections from Latin American Indian cultures.

598. _____, ed. and comp. *Technicians of the sacred*. Garden City, N.Y.: Doubleday, 1968. xxx, 520 p.

Well-annotated study and selection of so-called "primitive" poetry from Asia, Africa, America, and Oceania. Includes the Aztec poem, "The flight of Quetzalcoatl" (pp. 92-97), and other Latin American Indian poems and songs.

599. Roys, Ralph L., ed. and tr. *Ritual of the Bacabs; a book of Maya incantations*. Norman: Univ. of Oklahoma Pr., 1965. 193 p.

600. Stephan, Ruth, ed. and intro. *The singing mountaineers: Songs and tales of the Quechua people*. Comp. and tr. [into Spanish] José María Arguedas. Tr. [into English] Angel Flores, Kate Flores, and Ruth Stephan. Austin: Univ. of Texas Pr., 1957. 203 p. (London: Nelson, 1957; rpt. Univ. of Texas Pr., 1971)

A very valuable collection of Quechua folklore. Notes on the texts by Arguedas, a noted authority.

601. Strand, Mark, tr. *18 poems from the Quechua*. Cambridge, Mass.: Halty Ferguson, 1971. 29 p.

Short, lyric poems which complement those of *The singing mountaineers*. See No. 600.

B. Spanish Chronicles of the New World: A Selected Reading List of Works in English Translation

602. Arriaga, Pablo Joseph [José] de. *The extirpation of idolatry in Peru*. Ed. and tr. L. Clark Keating. Lexington, Kentucky: Univ. of Kentucky Pr., 1968. 192 p.

Based on manuscript of 1621. Includes a glossary of Quechua words.

603. Benavente, Fray Toribio de ("Motolinía"). *Motilinía's history of the Indians of New Spain*. Tr. Francis B. Steck. Washington, D.C.: Academy of American Franciscan History, 1961. 358 p.*

(from *Historia de los indios de Nueva España*)
Pseudonym means "the poor one," a term which is indicative of the author's sympathetic attitude. He opposed Las Casas, however, concerning the conversion of the Indians.

604. [Carrió de la Vandera, Alonso] Concolorcorvo. *El lazarillo: A guide for inexperienced travelers between Buenos Aires and Lima*. Tr. Walter D. Kline. Intro. Richard A. Mazarra. Foreword Irving A. Leonard. Bloomington, Indiana: Indiana Univ. Pr., 1965. 315 p. illus.*

(original title: *El lazarillo de ciegos caminantes*, 1775 or 1776)

Long believed to have been written by the Indian Calixto Bustamente Carlos Inca, but now attributed to the Spanish stage post inspector Carrió de la Vandera. Not chronicles of discovery, but lively, somewhat picaresque travel accounts.

605. Las Casas, Bartolomé de. *Bartolomé de Las Casas: A selection of his writings*. Ed. George Sanderlin. New York: Knopf, 1971. x, 209 p. bibliog.*

606. _____. *History of the Indies*. Tr. and ed. Andrée M. Collard. New York: Harper and Row, 1971. xxvi, 302 p. bibliog.

An edited version of *Historia de las Indias*, completed sometime after 1560, but not published until 1875.

607. Las Casas, Bartolomé de. *The tears of the Indians; being an historical and true account of the cruel massacres and slaughters of above twenty millions of innocent people committed by the Spaniards in the islands of Hispaniola, Cuba, Jamaica. . . . As also, in the continent of Mexico, Peru, and other places of the West Indies, to the total destruction of those countries*. Tr. John Phillips. Facs. rpt. of English edition of 1656. Stanford, California: Academic Reprints, 1953. 134 p.*

(original title: *Brevíssima relación de la destrucción de las Indias*, 1552)

Used by Spain's enemies to create the famous "Black Legend."

608. _____. *'Tears of the Indians', by Bartolomé de las Casas, and 'The life of Las Casas,' by Sir Arthur Helps*. Intro. Lewis Hanke.

Williamstown, Mass.: J. Lilburne, 1970. xviii, 84 p.; xix, 292 p.*

Reprints of two works. The former is a reprint of Phillips' trans. of *Brevíssima relación de la destrucción de las Indias* (tr. 1656). The latter is a reprint of the original edition (1896).

609. Cieza de León, Pedro. *The Incas of Pedro Cieza de León*. Tr. Harriet de On5is. Ed. and intro. Victor Wolfgang von Hagen. Norman: Univ. of Oklahoma Pr., 1959. lxxx, 397 p.

Trans. of part 2 of *La crónica del Perú* (1873), written during the middle part of the sixteenth century. One of the best written and most objective of the chronicles.

610. _____. *The travels of Pedro Cieza de León, 1532-50*. Tr. Clements R. Markham. Hakluyt Soc. Works, No. 33, 1864. lvii, 438 p. (rpt. New York: Burt Franklin, 1963)

Trans. of part 1 of *La crónica del Perú* (1553).

611. Columbus, Christopher. *The four voyages of Christopher Columbus. . . .* Ed. John Michael Cohen. Harmondsworth & Baltimore: Penguin, 1969. 320 p. paper

612. _____. *Four voyages to the New World: Letters and selected documents*. Tr. and ed. R. H. Major. Intro. John E. Fagg. New York: Corinth Books, 1961. 240 p. paper

Originally translated in 1847.

613. Cortés, Hernando. *Conquest: Dispatches of Cortés from the New World*. Ed. Harry M. Rosen. Intro. and commentaries Irwin R. Blacker.

New York: Grosset and Dunlap, 1962. 269 p. illus. paper*

For the general reader. Some abridgement of the *Cartas de relación* (1519-1526).

614. _____. *Five letters, 1519-1526.* Tr. J. Bayard Morris New York: Norton, 1962 388 p. paper (rpt. of 1928 edition)

615. Díaz del Castillo, Bernal. *The conquest of New Spain.* Ed., tr. and intro. J[ohn] M[ichael] Cohen. Harmondsworth & Baltimore: Penguin, 1963. 412 p. paper

Trans. of foot soldier Díaz del Castillo's lively *Verdadera historia de la conquista de la Nueva España*, published posthumously in 1632.

Revised ed., eliminating excess repetition. Uses modern punctuation.

616. Díaz del Castillo, Bernal. *The discovery and conquest of Mexico: 1517-1521.* Edited from the only exact copy of the original manuscript. . . . Tr. and intro. A. P. Maudslay. Intro. Irving A. Leonard. New York: Noonday Pr., 1965. xxx, 478 p. paper (rpt. of 1956 abridged edition [New York: Farrar, Straus and Cudahy] of Maudslay's English trans., 1908-1916)

The Maudslay translation is in turn based on Genaro García's Mexican edition (1904).

617. Fuentes, Patricia de, ed. and tr. *The Conquistadors: First person accounts of the conquest of Mexico.* Pref. Howard F. Cline. New York: Orion, 1963. xxii, 250 p. bibliog.*

618. Garcilaso de la Vega, el Inca. *The Florida of the Inca: A History of the Adelantado Hernando de Soto.*

Tr. and ed. John Grier Varner and Jeannette Johnson Varner. Austin: Univ. of Texas Pr., 1951. 655 p.

(original title: *La Florida del Inca*, 1605)

A novel-like account of Hernando de Soto's travels.

619. _____. *The Incas: The 'Royal Commentaries' of the Inca Garcilaso de la Vega, 1539-1616.* Tr. María Jolas, from the critical annotated French ed. of Alain Gheerbrant. Intro Alain Gheerbrant. New York: Orion Pr., 1961. 432 p. bibliog. illus. (rpt. New York: Avon, 1971. 447 p. paper)*

An annotated edition of *Comentarios reales que tratan del origen de los incas* (1609). From the origin of the Incas to Atalhualpa's death.

620. _____. *The Royal Commentaries of Peru.* Tr. Harold V. Livermore. Intro. Arnold Toynbee. Austin: Univ. of Texas Pr., 1966. 2 vols.*

Trans. of the two parts of the history by the hemisphere's first mestizo writer: *Comentarios reales que tratan del origen de los incas* (1609) and *Historia general del Perú* (1617).

621. López de Gómara, Francisco. *Cortes: The life of the Conqueror of Mexico by his secretary Francisco López de Gómara.* Tr. and ed. Lesley Byrd Simpson. Berkeley: Univ. of California Pr., 1966. xxvi, 425 p. (rpt. 1966, paper)

(from *Historia de la conquista de México*, the 2nd pt. of *Historia general de las Indias* (1578)

Selections are chosen which emphasize the exploits and character of

Cortés. In contrast to López de Gómara, Bernal Díaz del Castillo stressed the role of the common soldiers. See No. 615, No. 616.

622. Núñez Cabeza de Vaca, Alvar. *Adventures in the unknown interior of America*. Tr. Cyclone Covey. New York: Collier Books, 1962.

623. Sahagún, Fray Bernardino de. *Florentine Codex: General History of the things of New Spain*. Tr. Arthur Anderson and Charles Dibble (from the original Aztec). Salt Lake City, Utah: Univ. of Utah Pr. for School of American Research, Santa Fe, N. M., 1951-1963. 12 books in 11 vols.

His *Historia general de las cosas de Nueva España* was originally written in the Mexican dialect, and later rewritten in Spanish. This document is of great value as a source of ethnographic and folkloric information concerning the Aztecs.

624. Zárate, Agustín de. *The discovery and conquest of Peru*. Tr. J[ohn] M[ichael] Cohen. Harmondsworth & Baltimore: Penguin, 1968. 279 p. paper*

Trans. of the first 4 books of *Historia del descubrimiento y conquista del Perú* (1555).

It also contains translations of other chroniclers, such as Pedro Cieza de León, Garcilaso de la Vega, el Inca, and José de Acosta, in order to provide a more panoramic view of the conquest of Peru.

Index of Authors

Camps, David,   20

Canales, Nemesio R.,   2

Cancela, Arturo,   31

Cané, Luis,   49

Cantón, Wilberto L.,   49

Carballido, Emilio,   7, 76, 79, 166, 375

Cardenal, Ernesto,   3, 8, 40, 44, 57, 60, 346, 347, 411, 412

Cárdenas, Rolando,   18

Cardona Peña, Alfredo,   8

Cardoso, Onelio Jorge,   4, 5, 22, 29

Cardozo y Aragón, Luis,   44, 49

Cardozo, Joaquim,   426, 428

Carneiro, André,   428

Carneiro, Cecílio J.,   459

Caro, José Eusebio,   10, 52, 63, 70

Carpentier, Alejo,   3, 4, 9, 26, 29, 35, 63a, 136-138, 243

Carpio, Manuel,   69

Carranza, Eduardo,   49

Carrasco, M. Francisco,   30

Carrasquilla, Ricardo,   70

Carrasquilla, Tomás,   16

Carrénard, Adrian,   536

Carrera Andrade, Jorge,   11, 15, 44, 45, 49, 54, 55, 326-329

Carrera de Wever, Margarita,   59

Carrero, Jaime,   363

Carriès Lemaire, Emmeline,   533

Carrillo, Francisco,   37

Carrió de la Vandera, Alonso,   10

Carrión, Alejandro,   49

Carrión, Benjamín,   19

Carvajal, María Isabel; See: Carmen Lyra (pseud.)

Carvalho, Mariajosé de,   430

Carvalho, Ronald de,   427, 428, 430

Casal, Julián del,   11, 44, 56, 68, 70

Casas, Bartolomé de Las,   10

Casasús, Joaquín D.,   69

Casaus, Víctor,   39, 66

Casey, Calvert,   5

Casséus, Maurice,   536

Casséus, Pascal,   536

Castañeda Aragón, Gregorio,   19

Castellanos, Joaquín,   52

Castellanos, Rosario,   4, 7, 8, 167

Castilleros, R. E. J.,   30

Castillo, Abelardo,   29

Castillo, Laura del,   32

Castillo, Moisés,   30

Castillo, Otto René,   43, 57, 332

Castro, Fidel,   5

Castro, Héctor David,   10

Castro, Josué de,   460, 519

Castro Ríos, Andrés,   2

Castro Saavedra, Carlos,   8, 17

Castro Z., Oscar,   49

Ceide, Amelia,   59

Cervantes, Francisco,   65

Césaire, Aimé,   525-527, 530, 531, 535, 537, 575-579, 581, 582

Céspedes, Augusto,   19

Cevallos Larrea, Cristóbal,   330

Chalbaud, Ramón,   73

Chambertrand, Gilbert de,   526, 528, 534

Chan Marín, Carlos Francisco,   71

Chase, Alfonso,   71

Chassagne, Roland,   536

Chauvet, Marie,   539

Chávez, E. A.,   69

Chávez, Marco Fidel,   63a

Chevry, Arsène,   536

Chimie, Mário,   435

Chocano, José Santos,   1, 11, 13, 14, 44, 46, 52, 56, 68, 70, 352

Chumacero, Alí,   4, 7, 45, 65

Cieza de León, Pedro,   10

Cisneros, Antonio,   17, 37, 57, 353

Clavijero, Francisco Javier,   16

Claudio, Edwin,   2

Coicou, Massilon,   536

Colimon, Marie-Thérèse,   533

Colin, Eduardo,   69

Coll y Toste, Cayetano,   2, 21

Collazo, Miguel,   20

Coloane, Francisco,   114

Colón, Cristóbal,   10

Colón, Jesús,   2

Concepción, J. Agustín,   67

Concepción de Gracia, Gilberto,   2

Concolorcorvo,   10

Condé, José,   422

Contardo, Luis F.,   47, 52, 70

Conti, Haroldo Pedro,   32

Contín Aybar, Pedro René,   67

Mallea, Eduardo, 11, 22, 31, 91-93, 233, 234
Maluenda Labarca, Rafael, 11, 22
Mañach, Jorge, 19
Mancini, Jules, 19
Manco, Silverio, 72
Mangonés, Victor, 536
Manrique Cabrera, Francisco, 2
Manuel, Francisco, 62, 433
Maples Arce, Manuel, 65, 69
Mar, María del, 59
Maran, René, 547-550
Marcelin, Pierre, 541-545
Marechal, Leopoldo, 17, 49, 50
Margenat, Hugo, 12, 58
Marín, Juan, 19, 35, 370
Marín, Pachín, 2
Marín, Ramón Julia, 12
Marín del Solar, Mercedes, 52
Mariño, José Julán, 68
Marins, Francisco. 469
Mariscal, Ignacio, 69
Mármol, José, 10, 53, 62, 94
Marqués René, 3, 6, 8, 11, 12, 29, 79, 380
Márquez Campos, Alfredo, 180
Márquez Salas, Antonio, 8
Marré, Luis, 5, 39, 66
Marrero Núñez, Julio, 2
Marroquín, Lorenzo, 129
Martán Góngora, Helcías, 63a
Martes de Oca, Ignacio, 69
Martí, José, 11, 14, 44, 56, 63, 397
Martínez, Miguel Gerónimo, 69
Martínez Bilbao, Oscar, 121
Martínez Cáceres, Arturo, 250
Martínez Capó, Juan, 2
Martínez de la Vega, Pepe, 36
Martínez de Navarrete, José Manuel, 61
Martínez Estrada, Ezequiel, 44, 384
Martínez Moreno, Carlos, 17, 24, 32
Martínez Queirolo, José, 75
Martínez y Vela, Bartolomé, 16
Martínez Zuviría, Gustavo A.; See: Hugo Wast (pseud.)
Martos, Marco, 37
Marugg, Tip, 526, 554

Matas, Julio, 73
Matilla, Alfredo, 58
Matos Paoli, Francisco, 2, 58
Matto de Turner, Clorinda, 10, 197
Maya, Rafael, 49
Mayard, Constantin, 536
Mayard, Pierre, 536
Mayas Garbayo, Gonzalo, 21
Mayorga Rivas, Román, 52
Medeiros, Antônio Pinto de, 428
Medeiros e Albuquerque, José de, 420
Medina Vidal, Jorge, 71
Médiz Bolio, Antonio, 69, 251
Meireles, Cecília, 59, 60, 426-428, 430-432, 434
Mejía González, Luis, 60
Mejía Sánchez, Ernesto, 8
Meléndez, Concha, 2, 52
Meléndez, Juan, 19
Meléndez Muñoz, Miguel, 2
Melgar, Mariano, 63
Mello, Thiago de, 57
Melo Neto, João Cabral de, 415, 426-428, 430, 431
Mendes, Murilo, 426-429, 431
Méndez, Angel Luis, 58
Méndez, Francisco, 49
Méndez Ballester, Manuel, 2
Méndez Calzada, Enrique, 11
Méndez Dorich, Rafael, 49
Méndez Pereira, Octavio, 30
Mendive, Rafael María de, 38, 70
Menén Desleal, Alvaro, 75
Menéndez, Miguel Angel, 181
Menéndez Alberdi, Adolfo, 39
Menéndez Leal, Alvaro; See: Menén Desleal, Alvaro (pseud.)
Meneses, Guillermo, 22
Meneses, Porfirio, 8
Mera, Juan León, 10
Mercado, José, 2
Meruelo González, Anisia, 63a
Meyer, Augusto, 428, 430
Mieses Burgos, Franklin, 67
Milanés y Fuentes, José Jacinto, 10, 38
Milano, Dante, 428
Millán, Gonzalo, 17

Index of English Titles

Index of Original Titles

Index of Countries

Argentina 1, 3, 4, 8, 10, 11, 13-17, 19, 21, 22, 24-27, 29, 31-33, 35, 36, 40, 41, 43, 44, 46, 48-50, 52, 53, 55-57, 59, 62-64, 68, 70-76, 78-105, 214-235, 264-275, 368, 369, 382-392

Bolivia 3, 11, 13, 14, 16, 19, 21, 22, 44, 46, 49, 52, 56, 57, 59, 62, 106, 107

Brazil 4, 14-16, 26, 49, 57, 59, 62, 63a, 70, 79, 415-524

Chile 3, 4, 8, 10, 11, 13-19, 21, 22, 26-29, 31, 32, 35, 36, 40, 41, 44, 46-49, 52, 54-57, 59, 62, 63, 68, 70, 71, 73-79, 108-126, 236-238, 276-313, 370-372, 393-396

Colombia 1, 3, 4, 8, 10, 11, 13-17, 19, 21-24, 26, 27, 29, 31, 36, 44, 46, 48, 49, 52, 55-57, 59, 62, 63, 63a, 68, 70, 73, 75-78, 127-130, 239, 240, 314, 315

Costa Rica 1, 8, 11, 13, 14, 16, 49, 52, 59, 68, 71, 131, 241, 242

Cuba 1, 3-6, 8-11, 14, 16, 19-21, 26-29, 31, 32, 35, 38-40, 42-45, 49, 52, 53, 55-57, 59, 62, 63, 63a, 66, 68, 70, 73, 78, 79, 132-143, 226, 243, 244, 316-324, 373, 397, 555-561

Dominican Republic 1, 9-11, 13, 14, 16, 26, 52, 57, 59, 63, 63a, 67, 70, 144, 325

Ecuador 1, 8, 10, 11, 13-15, 19, 22, 29, 35, 40, 44, 45, 49, 52, 54, 55, 57, 59, 62, 63, 71, 75, 78, 145-148, 326-331

El Salvador 3, 8, 11, 13, 14, 16, 40, 49, 52, 57, 59, 71, 75

French Guiana 527, 530, 531, 534, 535, 537, 562

Guadeloupe 528, 531, 534, 535, 537, 563-572

Guatemala 3, 8, 10, 11, 14, 16, 17, 19, 26, 29, 31, 43, 44, 49, 52, 57, 59, 70, 73, 75, 149-156, 244-246, 332, 374

Haiti 49, 57, 59, 525-527, 529-545, 573, 574

Honduras 10, 11, 14, 49, 52, 59, 157, 158

Martinique 525-528, 530, 531, 534, 535, 537, 546-553, 575-582

Mexico 1, 3, 4, 7, 8, 10, 11, 13-17, 19, 21-24, 26-29, 31, 32, 34-36, 40, 41, 44-46, 48, 49, 51-57, 59, 61-63, 65, 68-71, 73, 76, 78, 79, 159-193, 226, 248-254, 333-345, 375-379, 398-410

Netherlands Antilles 526, 554

Nicaragua 1, 3, 8, 11, 13-15, 21, 26, 29, 40, 42-46, 48, 49, 52, 56, 59, 60, 62, 63, 68, 255, 346-351, 411, 412

Panama 8, 11, 22, 30, 49, 52, 59, 63a, 71

Paraguay 3, 8, 10, 11, 14, 19, 26, 29, 52, 59, 74, 194

Peru 1, 3, 4, 8, 10, 11, 13-17, 19, 21-23, 26, 27, 29, 31, 33, 35, 37, 40-46, 49, 52, 55-57, 59, 62, 63, 68, 70, 78, 195-199, 256-258, 352-361

Puerto Rico 2, 3, 6, 8-12, 14, 21, 26, 29, 38, 41, 44, 49, 52, 57-59, 62,

143